Theory for Today's Musician

WORKBOOK

Second Edition

**Ralph Turek and
Daniel McCarthy**

 Routledge
Taylor & Francis Group

NEW YORK AND LONDON

First published 2014
by Routledge
711 Third Avenue, New York, NY 10017

and by Routledge
2 Park Square, Milton Park, Abingdon, Oxon OX14 4RN

Routledge is an imprint of the Taylor & Francis Group, an informa business

© 2014 Taylor & Francis

The right of Ralph Turek and Daniel McCarthy to be
identified as authors of this work has been asserted by them in
accordance with sections 77 and 78 of the Copyright, Designs
and Patents Act 1988.

ISBN 13: 978–0–415–66333–5 (pbk)

Typeset in Galliard and Swiss 721
by Florence Production Ltd, Stoodleigh, Devon, UK

Senior Commissioning Editor: Constance Ditzel
U.S. Textbook Development Manager: Rebecca Pearce
Assistant Editor: Denny Tek
Production Editor: Mhairi Bennett
Project Manager: Charlotte Hiorns
Marketing Manager: Amy Langlais
Text Design: Susan R. Leaper
Cover Design: Jayne Varney
Composition: Florence Production Ltd
Companion Website Designer: Natalya Dyer

Workbook *to Accompany*
Theory for Today's Musician

Contents

Preface

This workbook is a supplement to *Theory for Today's Musician,* second edition. Each chapter corresponds to a chapter in the text and has the same title. The material, which can be used for in-class work or for assignments, is of three basic types:

- Analytical and part-writing drills that focus on theoretical problems in abstract isolation.
- Analytical problems involving larger excerpts from the literature.
- Exercises involving the application of theoretical concepts through actual composition.

The exercises/assignments are grouped to correspond to the major divisions in each chapter, so it is not necessary to cover a chapter in its entirety before reinforcing ideas.

In most cases, space is provided for the answers. The pages are perforated so that they can be torn out and handed in. Between the in-chapter exercises in the text and those contained here, multiple approaches to any given theoretical concept are provided, and students should benefit from the many approaches to any given concept.

The authors would like to acknowledge Professors Randy Earles (Idaho State University), David Hanan (University of Central Oklahoma), and Elaine Rendler (George Mason University) and thank them for their keen eyes and useful feedback on the new edition of this workbook.

CHAPTER ONE
Assorted Preliminaries

A. Identify the modes and transpose each in the same clef to consist entirely of unaltered pitches ("white keys").

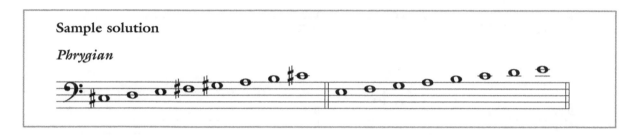

Sample solution

Phrygian

1 _____

2 _____

3 _____

4 _____

5 _____

6 _____

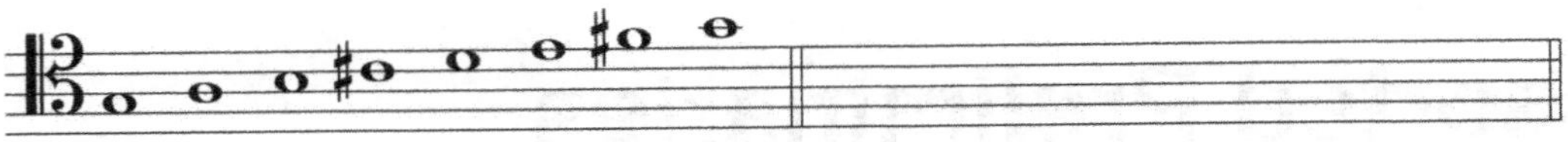

7 _____

8 _____

9 _____

10 _____

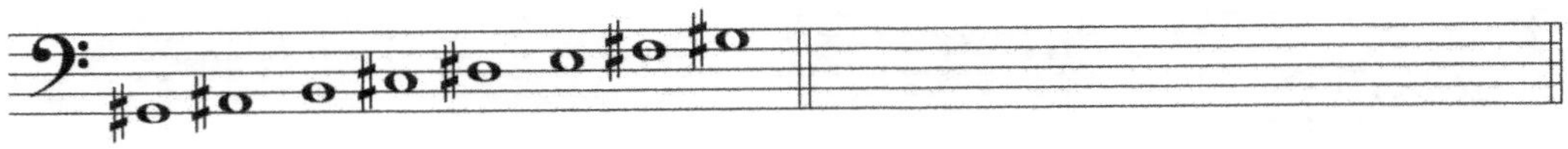

B. Add the accidental(s) needed to create the specified mode. Be careful to observe the clefs. Do not change the first pitch.

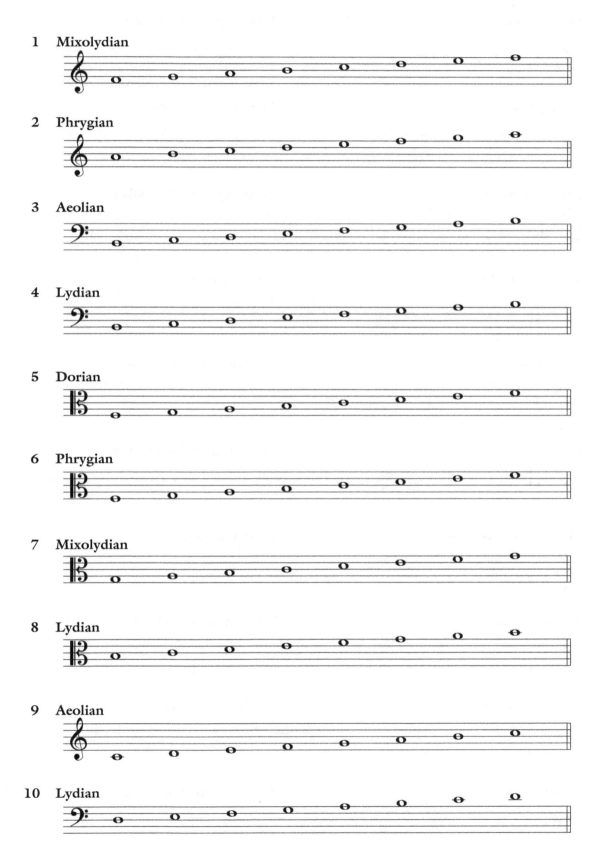

C. Write the requested modes beginning on the given final, adding accidentals where needed. Then show the key signature needed to change the mode as indicated.

1   **Dorian mode on:**   **To change to Phrygian:**

2   **Mixolydian mode on:**   **To change to Dorian:**

3   **Lydian mode on:**   **To change to Mixolydian:**

4   **Phrygian mode on:**   **To change to Lydian:**

5   **Aeolian mode on:**   **To change to Phrygian:**

6   **Phrygian mode on:**   **To change to Mixolydian:**

7   **Mixolydian mode on:**   **To change to Dorian:**

8   **Lydian mode on:**   **To change to Aeolian:**

9   **Dorian mode on:**   **To change to Lydian:**

10 **Mixolydian mode on:**   **To change to Phrygian:**

D. Identify the mode for each melody. Then, re-notate the melody on the blank staff, using the specified transposition and clef. (Note: If accidentals are present in the original version, they'll be necessary in your transposition as well.)

1 Mode _____

2 Mode _____

3   Mode _____

4   Mode _____

E.   Repeat the following two-measure melodic fragment, adding the accidentals needed to change the mode first to Lydian, then Mixolydian, then Dorian, then Aeolian, and finally Phrygian.

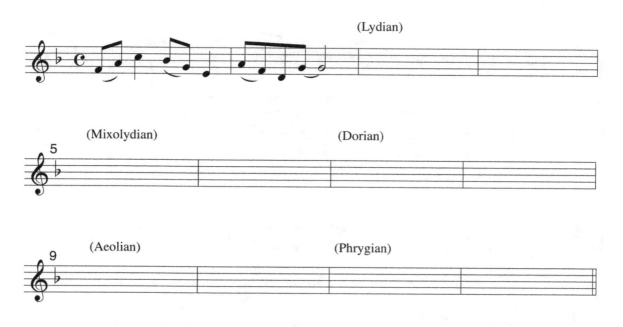

F.   Identify the mode of each melody. In which of these is there a rather clear hypermeter? Place an "S" (Strong) and "W" (Weak) above the measures to show this larger-level accentual pattern.

1   "Scarborough Fair" (English folk song)

Mode: _____ on E

2   Adele Adkins and Fraser T. Smith: "Set Fire to the Rain" 🔊

Mode: _____ on D

3   Debussy: String Quartet, op. 10 (first movement)

Mode: _____ on G

4   Danny Elfman: "Simpsons" Theme

Mode: _____ on D♭

5   Barry Mann, Cynthia Weil, Jerry Lieber, and Mike Stollar: "On Broadway"

Mode: _____ on E

6   Kabalevsky: Eighteen Pieces for Children, op. 27 (Sonatina) 🔊

Mode: _____ on A

G.   For the following passages, identify the way the beat is divided (into two or three parts), the way beats are grouped (into measures of three or four beats), give the meter classification (assume that duple includes quadruple), and identify the hypermeter.

1   Traditional: "Drink to Me Only with Thine Eyes" 🔊

Division of beat: 2__   3__

Grouping of beats (division of measure):   3__   4__

Meter classification:

    Simple duple __   Simple triple __

    Compound duple __   Compound triple __

Grouping of measures (Hypermeter):   2__   3__   4__

2 Ed Haley: "While Strolling Through the Park" 🔊

Division of beat: 2___   3___

Grouping of beats (division of measure):   3___   4___

Meter classification:

    Simple duple ___   Simple triple ___

    Compound duple ___   Compound triple ___

Grouping of measures (Hypermeter):   2___   3___   4___

CHAPTER TWO

Intervals

1.   IDENTIFYING AND SPELLING INTERVALS

1A. State the number of black keys spanned by the following white-key Intervals. Then, identify the interval.

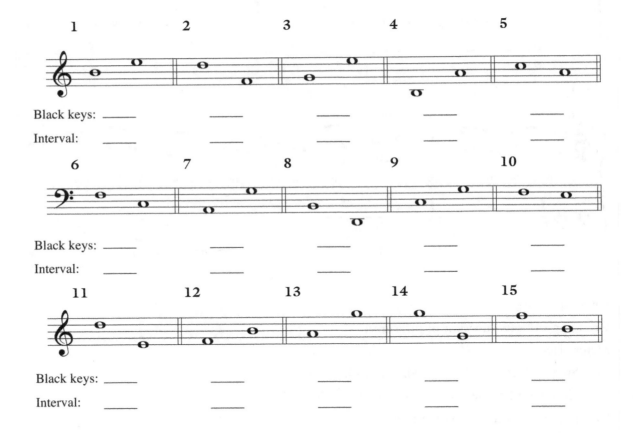

1B. Using Example 2-5 from your text and the chart that follows it as a reference, name each interval and its altered form. The intervals are unisons, fourths, fifths, or octaves.

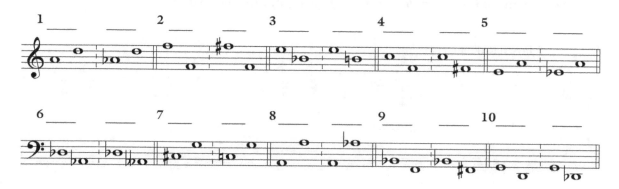

1C. Using Example 2-5 as a reference, name each interval and its altered form. The intervals are seconds, thirds, sixths, or sevenths.

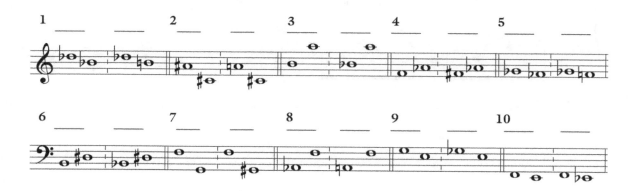

1D. Notate the requested pitches in the indicated clefs.

1 M3 above G♯4   2 m6 below E2   3 P4 above A3   4 M7 above F♯3 5 m3 below A♭4

6 +4 below C♯3   7 M6 above F♯5 8 M2 below E♭3 9 P5 above F♭3 10 m7 below D♯6

11 °7 above G3   12 °5 above E♭2 13 m6 above B♭2 14 M3 below A♭5 15 +4 below G3

1E. Indicate the size and quality of each interval in the left-hand melody that follows.

Schumann: *43 Klavierstücke für die Jugend,* op. 68, no. 10

Interval: ___ ___ ___ ___ ___ ___ ___

1F. Notate the intervals. Add sharps or flats required by the key. It may be helpful to complete this at the piano. One of the three thirds is given in **1**.

1   In E♭ : the three major thirds (the first is given)

2   In G: the five major seconds

3   In A: the six perfect fourths

4   In D♭ : the four minor thirds

5   In A♭ : the three minor sixths

6   In D: the four major sixths

7   In F: the two minor seconds

8   In E: the two major sevenths

9   In G♭ : the three major thirds

10   In B♭ : the four major sixths

1G. Regard the first pitch of each pair as the tonic of a major scale. (The second pitch might or might not be a member of the scale.) Write the intervening scale steps between the two pitches. Then, identify the interval, using the method described following text Example 2-6.

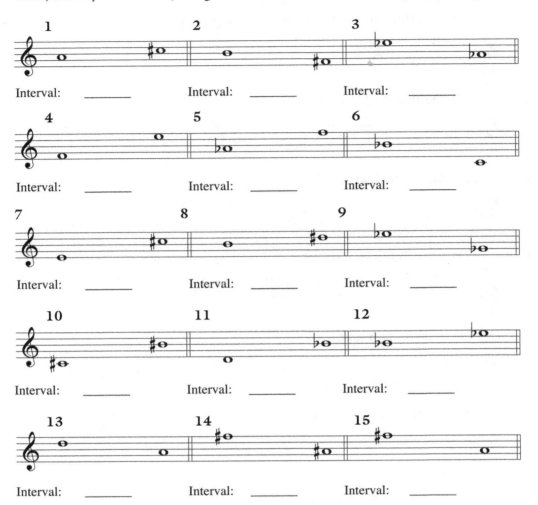

2. RELATED MATTERS

2A. Match the enharmonic intervals.

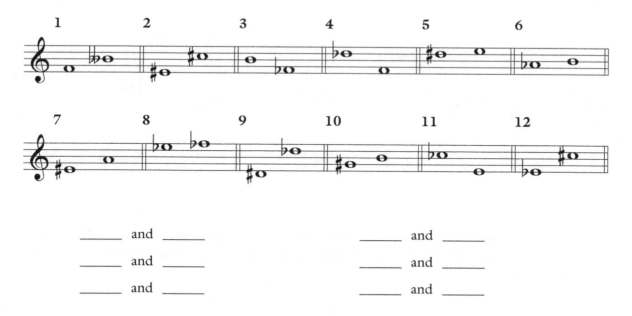

_____ and _____   _____ and _____

_____ and _____   _____ and _____

_____ and _____   _____ and _____

2B. Respell the following intervals enharmonically in two ways. At least one spelling should be a numeric value different from the original. Identify both intervals.

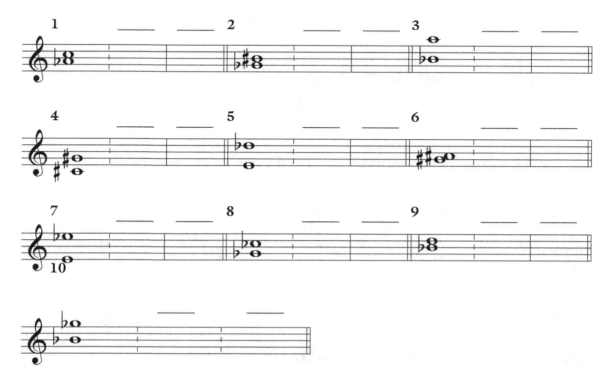

2C. Name the interval. Then, respell it enharmonically so that the numeric value and quality remain the same.

2D. Identify the following intervals. Then respell the *second* note in each interval enharmonically so that the sound remains the same but the numeric value and quality are different. Identify the new interval.

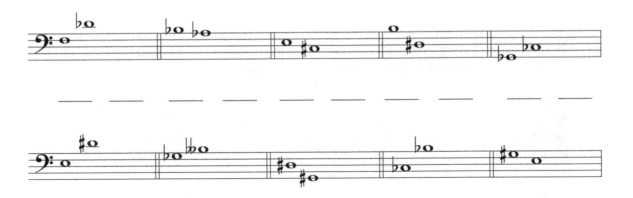

2E. Identify each interval. Then, invert the interval and name the inversion.

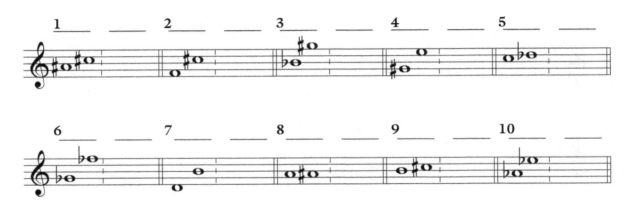

2F. Name the interval. Then, invert it in such a way that both pitches of the new interval remain on the staff (i.e. do not require ledger lines). Then, name the new interval.

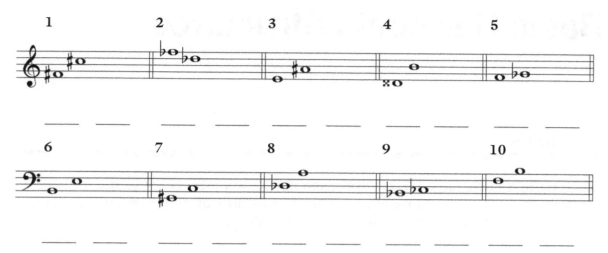

2G. Name the intervals in the following melody. Name compound intervals in their simple-interval form.

Eben Rexford and Hart Danks: "Silver Threads Among the Gold"

CHAPTER THREE
Basic Harmonic Structures

1. TRIADS

1A. Place an X in the blank beneath each chord that is *not* a triad. For those that are, place the letter name of the root in the blank and, on the bass-clef staff, restack the other two notes as a third and a fifth above it. (Eliminate octave doublings.)

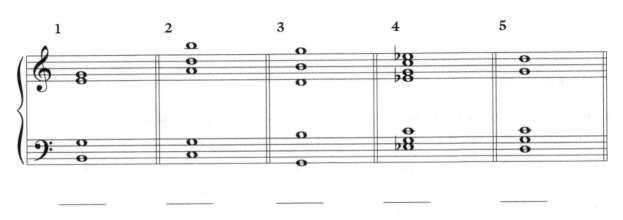

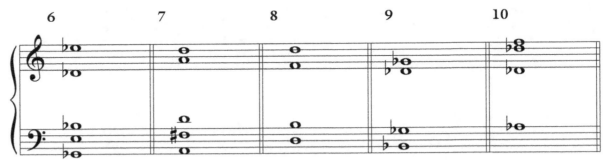

1B. Name the root and quality (M, m, o, +) of each triad.

Root: _____ _____ _____ _____ _____

Quality: _____

1C. Next to each chord, show the *single pitch alteration* that will create a triad of the quality indicated.

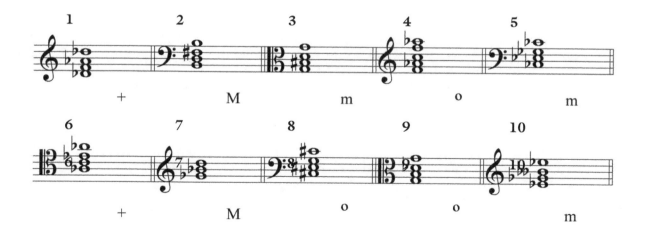

1D. Construct the indicated triads above the given pitches. (Take careful note of the clefs.)

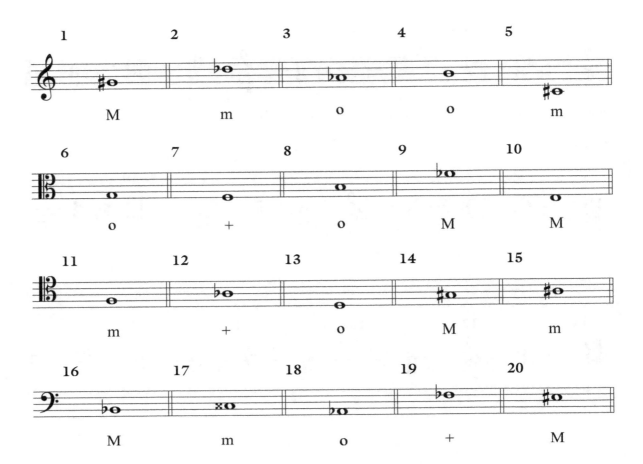

1E. Given M, m, +, or o, treat each pitch first as the root (R), then as the third (3), and finally as the fifth (5) of the triad, and construct the triad of the specified quality. Place the *root* lowest in the stack for all chords.

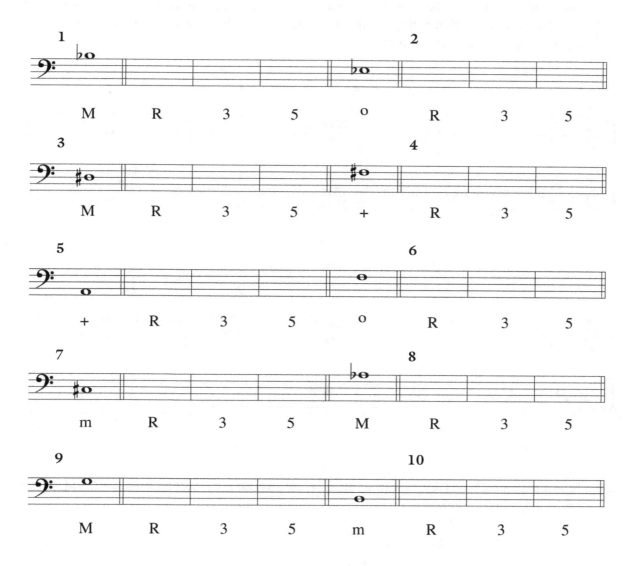

2. CHORD INVERSION

2A. Indicate the inversion of the chord *as given* (R = root position, 1 = first inversion, 2 = second
inversion). Then place the root of the triad in the lowest position, and stack the other chord
members above it, eliminating doubled tones. (It may be necessary to transpose certain
members of the chord by an octave.)

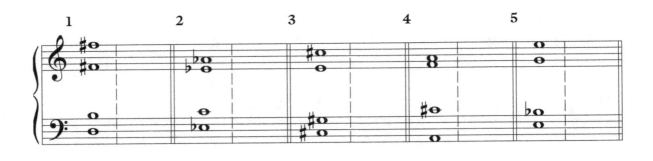

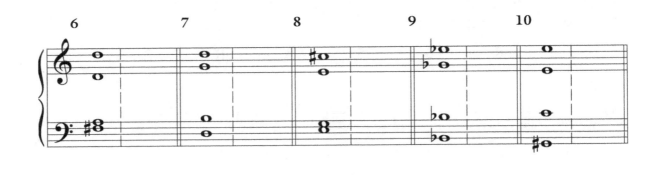

2B. Indicate the inversion (R = root position, 1 = first inversion, 2 = second inversion), and quality
(M, m, o, +) of the triads.

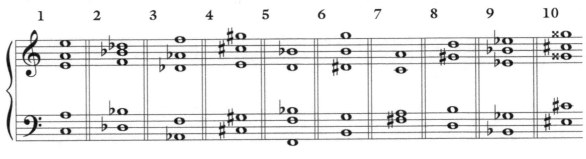

Inversion: _____ _____ _____ _____ _____ _____ _____ _____ _____ _____

Quality: _____ _____ _____ _____ _____ _____ _____ _____ _____ _____

2C. Construct three triads of the same quality that employ the given pitch as a chord member. Retain the given pitch as the lowest sounding member of the triad. The first triad is to be in root position (R), the second in first inversion (1), and the third in second inversion (2).

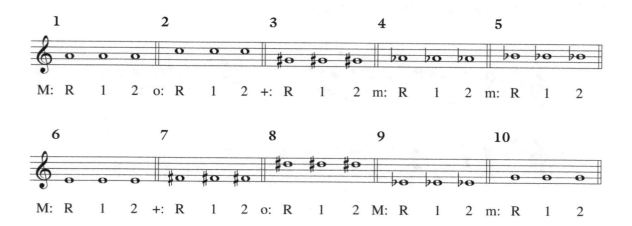

2D. Write the following triads in the inversion indicated. The given note is to be the lowest pitch in the chord.

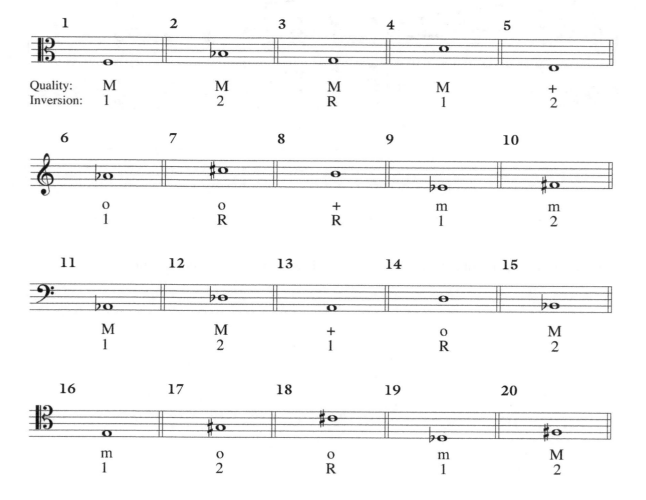

2E. Identify the root, quality, and inversion of each triad. Place an X in the blanks where a triad is incomplete (containing only two of its three members).

Haydn: Piano Sonata no. 17 (Menuetto)* 🔊

Root: _____   _____   _____   _____   _____   _____   _____

Quality: _____   _____   _____   _____   _____   _____   _____

Inversion: _____   _____   _____   _____   _____   _____   _____

_____   _____   _____   _____   _____   _____   _____

_____   _____   _____   _____   _____   _____   _____

_____   _____   _____   _____   _____   _____   _____

*This work is of doubtful authenticity. It has not been assigned a Hoboken number.

3. SEVENTH CHORDS

3A. Classify the seventh chords as: MM7; Mm7; mm7; ø7; or o7

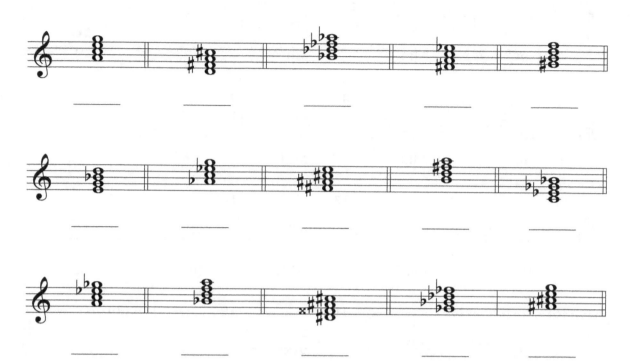

3B. Identify the quality and inversion (R, 1, 2, or 3) of the seventh chords.

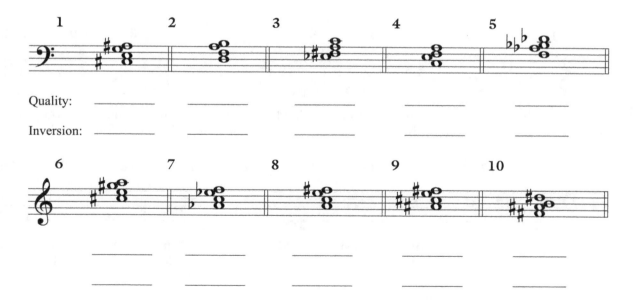

Quality: _____ _____ _____ _____ _____

Inversion: _____ _____ _____ _____ _____

3C. Construct the seventh chord above the given root.

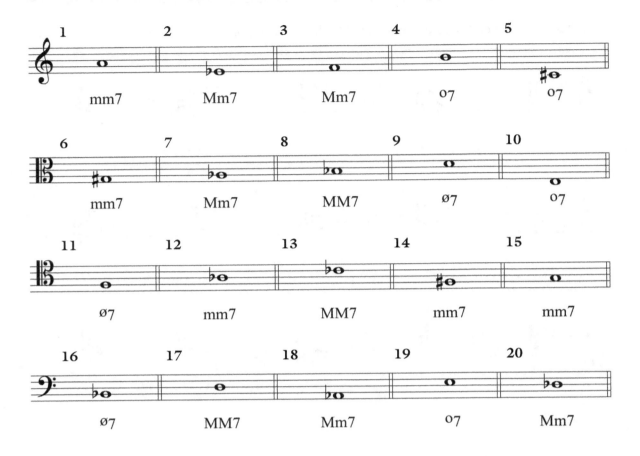

3D. Construct *above the given pitch* a seventh chord of the quality and inversion requested.

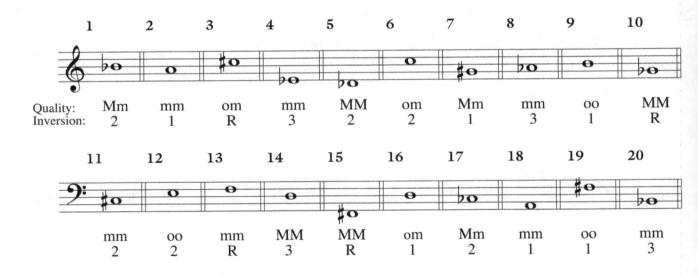

3E. Construct the root-position seventh chords specified. The given pitch is designated as either the root (R), third (3), fifth (5), or seventh (7). You'll need to add notes above and/or below it to complete the chord.

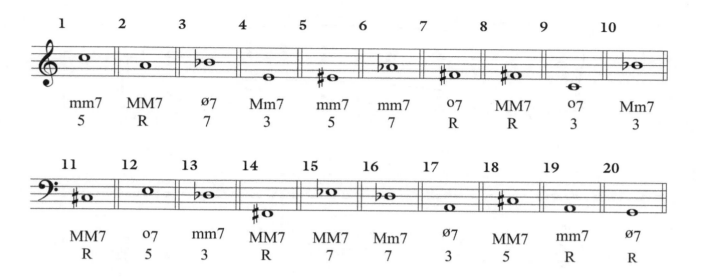

3F. In the excerpt that follows, identify the root, quality, and inversion of each triad or seventh chord.

Bill Evans and Gene Lees: "Waltz for Debby" 🔊))

Root: ___ ___ ___ ___ ___ ___   _____

Quality: ___ ___ ___ ___ ___ ___   _____

Inversion: ___ ___ ___ ___ ___ ___   _____

* This C was changed from D for the purpose of making this passage suitable for chord identification at this time. **Disregard the circled pitches in identifying this chord.

3G. 1.   Identify the root, quality, and inversion of each triad or seventh chord in the following
          song.

     2.   Notate a new bass as it would appear in the absence of inversions. Compare and contrast
          this bass line with the given one. Which do you prefer, and why?

Cocrad Kocher: "Dix" 🔊

Root: _ _ _ _ _ _ _ _ _ _ _ _ _ _ _ _ _

Quality: _ _ _ _ _ _ _ _ _ _ _ _ _ _ _ _ _

Inversion: _ _ _ _ _ _ _ _ _ _ _ _ _ _ _ _ _

CHAPTER FOUR

Musical Shorthand: Lead Sheets and Figured Bass

1. LEAD-SHEET NOTATION

1A. Spell the triads indicated by the lead-sheet symbols.

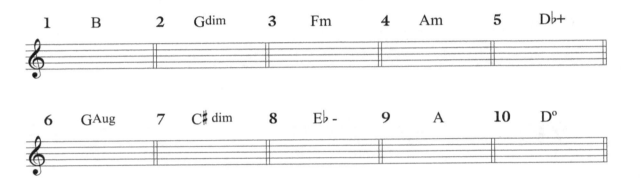

1B. Show the lead-sheet symbol for each triad.

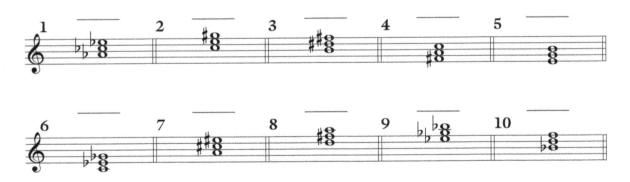

1C. Spell the seventh chords indicated by the lead-sheet symbols.

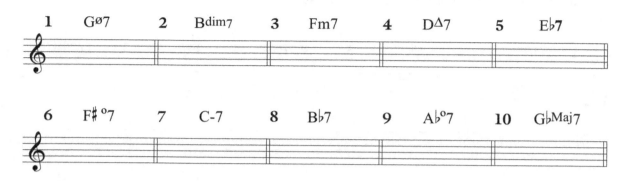

1 Gø7 2 Bdim7 3 Fm7 4 DΔ7 5 E♭7

6 F#°7 7 C-7 8 B♭7 9 A♭°7 10 G♭Maj7

1D. Provide lead-sheet symbols for the following chords.

1 ____ 2 ____ 3 ____ 4 ____ 5 ____

6 ____ 7 ____ 8 ____ 9 ____ 10 ____

1E. Show the lead-sheet symbol for each seventh chord.

1F. Construct the chords indicated by the lead-sheet symbols. Place the bass note in the bass clef and the rest of the chord on the treble-clef staff.

1   G/F   2   E♭7   3   Aø7/E♭   4   F♯/E   5   D♭Maj7

6   C♯°7/E   7   B -7   8   Eø7/D   9   A♭7   10   Dm/F

1G. Show the expanded lead-sheet symbol that represents both the chord type and the bass note.

1

2

Like a fanfare

1H. This timeless glee-club favorite tells the macabre tale of Clementine, a young woman who lived
      "in a cavern in a canyon" and managed to fall into the "foaming brine" while her father was
      prospecting. Add lead-sheet symbols that express both the chord types and bass line. You should
      be able to do so using the symbols for seventh chords and the expanded lead-sheet notation
      explained earlier in the chapter. Disregard the non-chord tones (circled).

Percy Montross: "Clementine"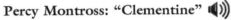

Arr. R. T.

11.   Add the lead-sheet symbols that express both the chord types and bass line. Analyze only the chords that fall directly beneath the blanks, and disregard circled tones.

Traditional: "Danny Boy"

2. FIGURED-BASS NOTATION

2A. Above the given bass note construct the triad that is indicated by the figures. Then, identify the triad as major (M), minor (m), augmented (+), or diminished (o).

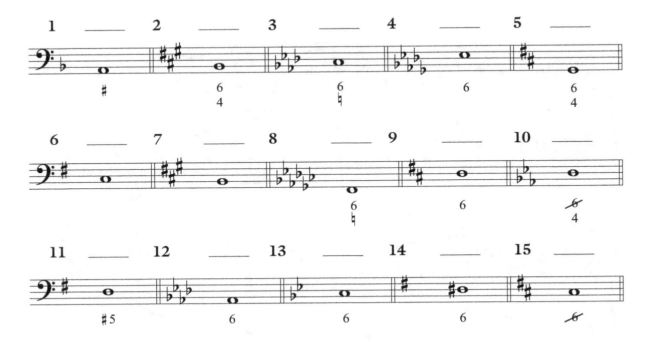

2B. In the blanks, add the symbol needed to complete the figured bass that would represent the given chords. Observe the key signature, and show accidentals in the figures where necessary.

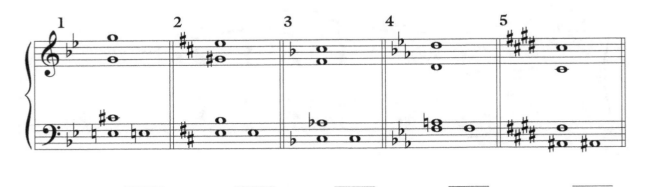

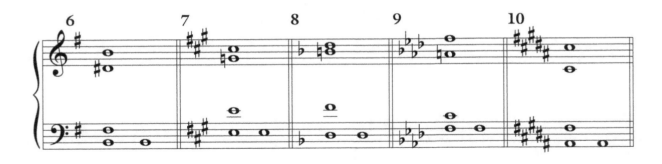

2C. Add the pitches necessary to form a complete triad above each figured-bass note. Play each example to become familiar with the sound of the harmonies.

2D. Add the pitches necessary to form complete triads above each bass note. Then, place the correct lead-sheet symbol in the blanks above the notes.

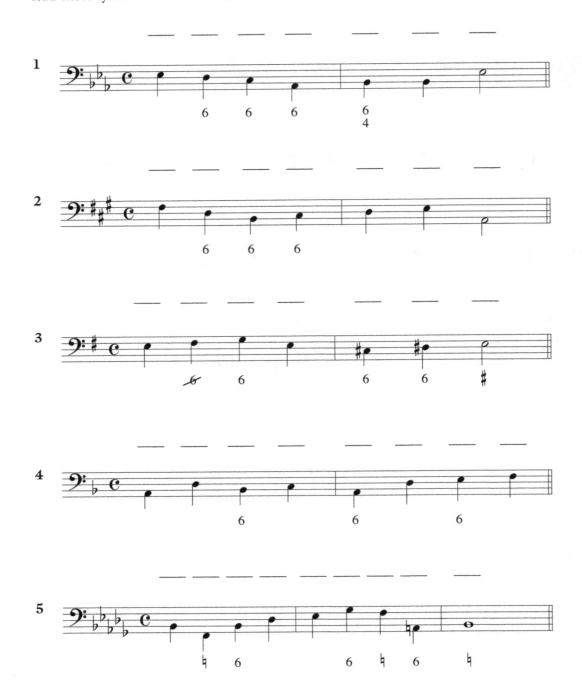

2E. In the blanks, figure the bass to represent each chord. By convention, no figures need to be added beneath root-position triads. Leave these blanks empty.

1 **J.S. Bach: "O du Liebe meiner Liebe" (adaptation)** 🔊

a: ___ ___ ___ ___ ___ ___ ___ ___ ___ ___

2 **J.S. Bach: "Nur mein Jesus ist mein Leben"** 🔊

g: ___ ___ ___ ___ ___ ___ ___ ___ ___ ___ ___ ___ ___ ___ ___

2F. In the blanks above each chord, give the lead-sheet symbol. Beneath the chords, supply the figured bass symbol that, together with the bass note, would reflect the chord.

Bourgeois: "Doxology"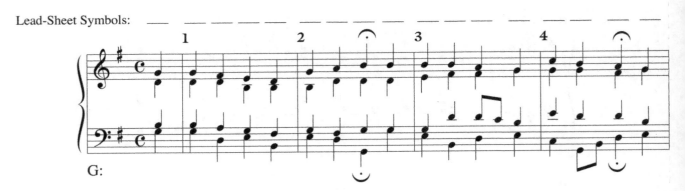

Lead-Sheet Symbols:

G:

Figured Bass:

CHAPTER FIVE

Harmonies of the Major and Minor Scales

1. DIATONIC CHORDS

1A. Write the indicated triads using accidentals rather than key signatures

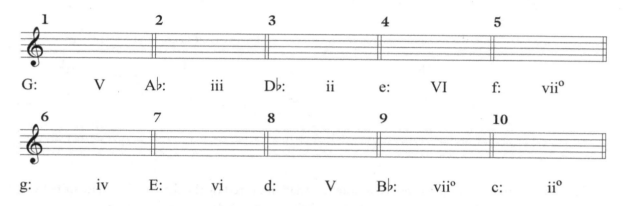

1B. Add the key signature, and then illustrate the indicated triads in root position. Be sure to observe the clef signs.

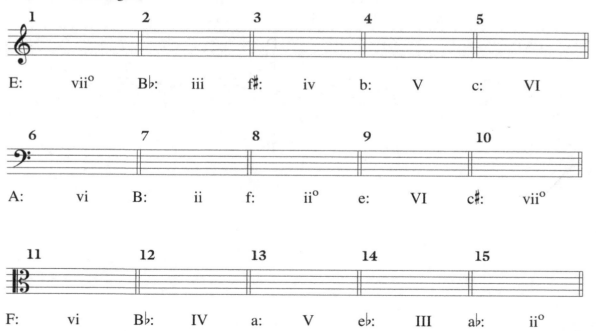

1C. Using Examples 5-2 and 5-4 from your text as references, show the function of each triad in the keys indicated by placing the appropriate Roman-numeral symbol in the blanks. If the triad is *not* diatonic in a key, place an X in that blank. (Regard the alternative minor-key harmonies as diatonic.)

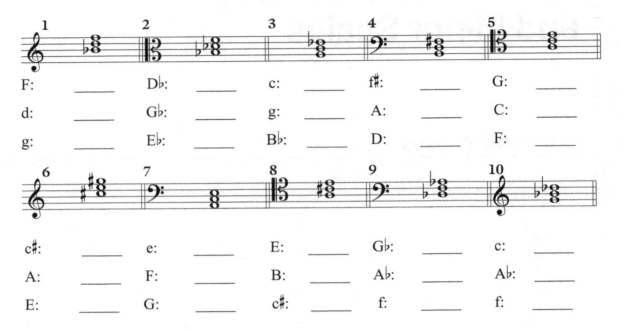

F: ____	Db: ____	c: ____	f#: ____	G: ____
d: ____	Gb: ____	g: ____	A: ____	C: ____
g: ____	Eb: ____	Bb: ____	D: ____	F: ____

c#: ____	e: ____	E: ____	Gb: ____	c: ____
A: ____	F: ____	B: ____	Ab: ____	Ab: ____
E: ____	G: ____	c#: ____	f: ____	f: ____

1D. Construct above the given bass note the triad indicated by the figures. Then, identify by Roman numeral (with superscript to show inversion, if needed) its function in the key.

Ab: _____	eb: _____	D: _____	F#: _____	Eb: _____

f: _____	bb: _____	E: _____	a: _____	g: _____

1E. Regarding each pitch as a root, construct the triad as it would normally appear in the indicated keys. For minor keys, use the most common minor-key harmonies, as explained in the chapter. Then, identify the triad's function in each key by placing Roman numerals in the blanks.

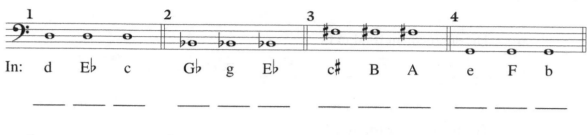

In: d   Eb   c   Gb   g   Eb   c#   B   A   e   F   b

____   ____   ____   ____   ____   ____   ____   ____   ____   ____   ____   ____

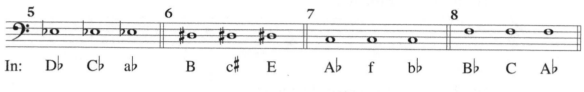

In: Db   Cb   ab   B   c#   E   Ab   f   bb   Bb   C   Ab

____   ____   ____   ____   ____   ____   ____   ____   ____   ____   ____   ____

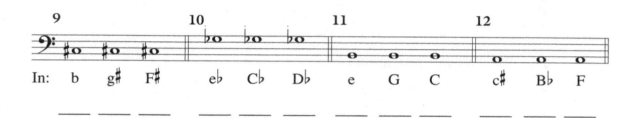

In: b   g#   F#   eb   Cb   Db   e   G   C   c#   Bb   F

____   ____   ____   ____   ____   ____   ____   ____   ____   ____   ____   ____

1F. Add the key signature and notate:

   1   The three major triads in Bb

   2   The two minor triads in f# (harmonic form)

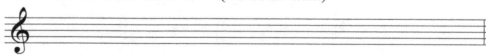

   3   The two diminished triads in g (harmonic form)

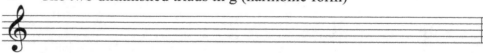

   4   The two diminished triads in eb (harmonic form)

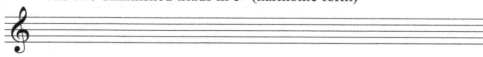

continued

5   The three minor triads in A♭

6   The submediant triad in f

7   The three major triads in d

8   The dominant in g (descending form)

9   The three minor triads in F♯

10   The augmented triad in the relative minor of E

1G. Identify by Roman numeral symbol the function of the following root-position seventh chords.

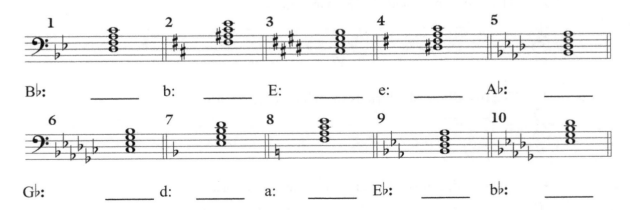

B♭: _____   b: _____   E: _____   e: _____   A♭: _____

G♭: _____   d: _____   a: _____   E♭: _____   b♭: _____

1H. Identify by Roman numeral and superscript the following seventh chords.

Eb: _____   Ab: _____   D: _____   e: _____   bb: _____

g: _____   a: _____   f#: _____   B: _____   A: _____

1I. Add the key signature and notate the seventh chords.

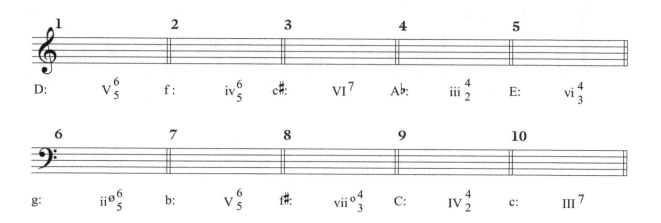

D: V^6_5 f: iv^6_5 c#: VI^7 Ab: iii^4_2 E: vi^4_3

g: $ii\text{ø}^6_5$ b: V^6_5 f#: $vii\text{o}^4_3$ C: IV^4_2 c: III^7

1J.   Provide a harmonic analysis of the following song. Most of the notes, but not all, are part of the underlying chords. The blanks are situated to appear beneath only those notes that comprise the chords.

Amanda McBroom: "The Rose" Arr. R.T.

2. FUNCTIONAL TONALITY

2A. Precede each of the given tonic triads with the triads that would create a descending-fifth series beginning on the mediant. Then, provide the Roman-numeral symbol for each triad in the blank beneath it.

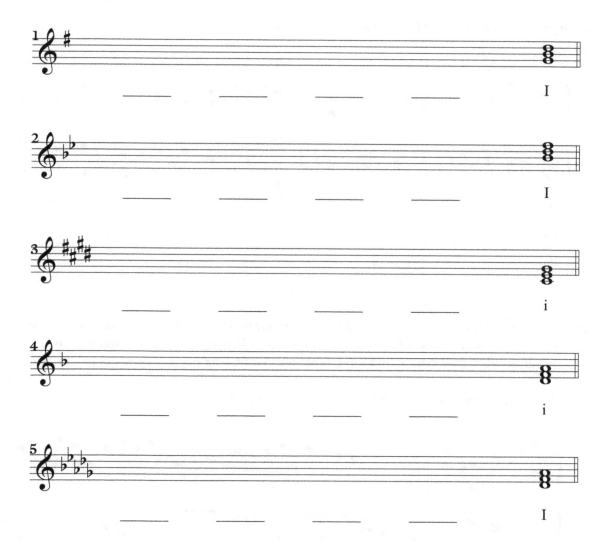

2B. In the blanks beneath the music, give a Roman numeral analysis and indicate the type of harmonic motion that occurs between the chords–progression (P), retrogression (R), or repetition (S for "same function"). Consider both a repeated chord and a *repeated function* (*i.e.* ii-IV, or V-viio) a harmonic repetition. (See textbook Examples 5-7 and 5-8.) No motion blanks follow tonic chords.

Bourgeois: "Doxology" ("Old 100th")

Key: ____

Analysis: __ ___ ___ ___ ___ ___ ___ ___ ___ ___ ___ ___ ___ ___ ___ ___

Motion: ___ ___ ___ ___   ___ ___ ___ ___ ___

2C. Provide harmonic analysis of the following excerpts. Disregard circled tones, as they are not part of the harmonies. Then, identify the motion between harmonies, using P, R, or S for progression, retrogression, and same function. No motion blanks follow tonic chords.

1   **Mozart: Piano Sonata K. 284 (third movement)**

Key: ____

Analysis: ____ ____ ____ ____ ____

Motion: ___ ___ ___ ___

2   J.S. Bach: "Jesu, meiner Seelen Wonne"

Key ____ : __ __ __ __ __ __ __ __ __ __ __ __ __ __

Motion: __ __ __ __

3   Schubert: Originaltanz, op. 9, no. 3

Key ____ :   __ __ __ __

Motion: __ __ __

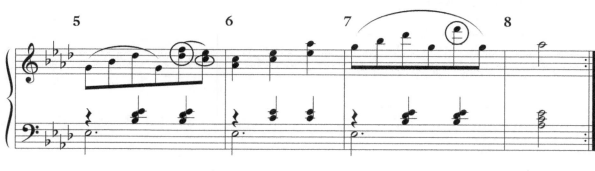

Key: _____   _____   _____   _____

Motion: _____

2D. Circle the tonic in each of the following chord successions. (There will be only one key in which all the chords are diatonic.) Using the letters <u>P</u>, <u>R</u>, and <u>S</u>, indicate the type of harmonic motion (<u>P</u>rogression, <u>R</u>etrogression, or <u>S</u>ame function) between the chords. Use an <u>X</u> to signify motion *from* the tonic.

1   G♭—e♭—c°7—F—b♭

_____

2   d—g—d—A—B♭

_____

3   C—a—D—e—C—D—G

_____

4   F—d—g—C—a—d—C

_____

5   E♭—A♭—f—B♭—g—c—B♭

_____

6   F♯—b—G—a♯°—b—e—F♯

_____

7   E—g♯—A—B—E—A—B

_____

8   C—D♭—b♭—g°—f—C—f

_____

2E. 1   Write a root-position chord that will create the specified harmonic motion *from* each given chord. In the blanks, provide harmonic analysis of both chords.

D: ____ P ____   Ab: ____ P ____   F: ____ R ____   g: ____ P ____   e: ____ S ____

2   Write a root-position chord that will create the specified harmonic motion *to* each given chord. Provide harmonic analysis of both chords.

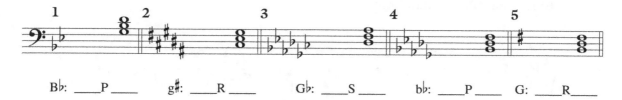

Bb: ____ P ____   g#: ____ R ____   Gb: ____ S ____   bb: ____ P ____   G: ____ R ____

2F.   Provide Roman-numeral analysis. Compare the harmonic patterns. Which of the patterns described in the text does each excerpt resemble?

1   **Keith Reid and Gary Brooker: "A Whiter Shade of Pale"**   Arr. R.T.

Key ____: ____   ____   ____   ____

2　Pachelbel: Canon in D (Assume root position chords)

D:　_____　_____　_____　_____　_____　_____　_____　_____

3　Billy Joel: "Piano Man"

It's　nine　o' - clock　on　a　Sat - ur - day.　　The

Key: _____

Analysis:　_____　_____　_____　_____

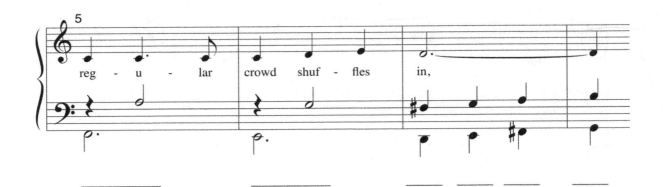

reg - u - lar　crowd　shuf - fles　in,

CHAPTER SIX

Cadences/Harmonic Rhythm

1. CADENCES

1A. The given chords form the standard cadences described in Chapter 6. In the blanks beneath, add the Roman-numeral chord symbols. In the blanks above, name the cadence (PAC or IAC, PC, HC, DC, or Phrygian HC).

1. Phrygian HC   2. DC   3. AC   4. DC   5. HC

f: iv⁶ V   A: IV I   E♭: V I   D: V VI   E: IV V

6. DC   7. AC   8. AC   9. HC   10. HC

a: V I   a: V I   c: V I   D♭: IV V   f♯: IV⁶ V

1B. Identify the key and cadence indicated by the lead-sheet symbols. Numbers 1 and 9 have two possible answers. You may find it helpful to refer to the Summary of Standard Cadences on page 90.

    1.   F—C   Key ___   Cadence _____

    2.   G°/B♭—A♭   Key ___   Cadence _____

    3.   D—Em   Key ___   Cadence _____

    4.   F—Gm   Key ___   Cadence _____

    5.   B♭/D—E♭   Key ___   Cadence _____

    6.   Em—Bm   Key ___   Cadence _____

    7.   A—B♭   Key ___   Cadence _____

    8.   Fm/A♭—G   Key ___   Cadence _____

    9.   A—E   Key ___   Cadence _____

  10.   C#—F#m   Key ___   Cadence _____

1C. Complete the chords suggested by the following figured basses. Then, provide a Roman numeral analysis. Finally, indicate the type of cadence: authentic, plagal, half, deceptive, or Phrygian half.

1D. Name a cadence that:

1. Ends on a G minor triad in the key of B♭:_____

2. Ends on a D major triad in the key of G: _____

3. Involves root movement from B to F♯ in F♯ minor: _____

4. Involves descending fifth root movement from G♯ in the key of C♯ minor: _____

5. Involves a descending bass from C to B in E minor: _____

1E. In the following passages:

1. Indicate the key.

2. Provide Roman numeral analysis.

3. Indicate the type of cadence.

Disregard circled tones.

1   J. S. Bach: "Schmucke dich, o liebe Seele"

Key____: __ __ __ ____ __ __ ____ __ __ __ __ __ __ __ ____ __

2   Brahms: *Hungarian Dance No. 5*

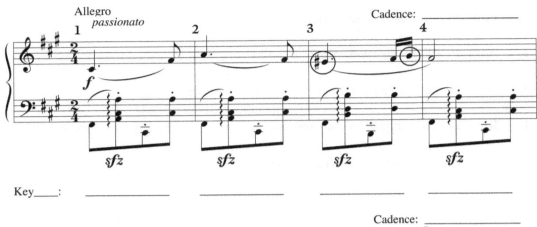

Key____: _____   _____   _____   _____

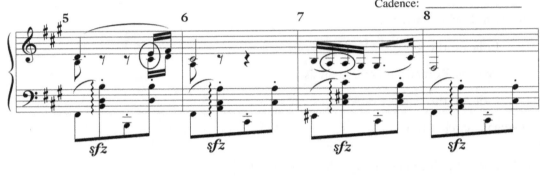

_____   _____   _____   _____

3   Traditional: "Amazing Grace"

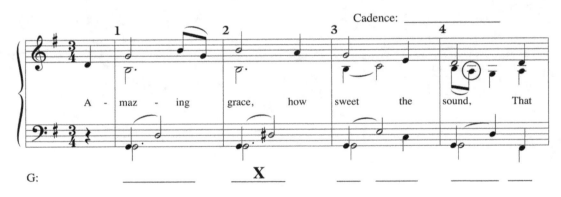

G: _____   X   _____   _____

X

4 Corelli: *Concerto Grosso*, op. 6, no. 8 (fourth movement)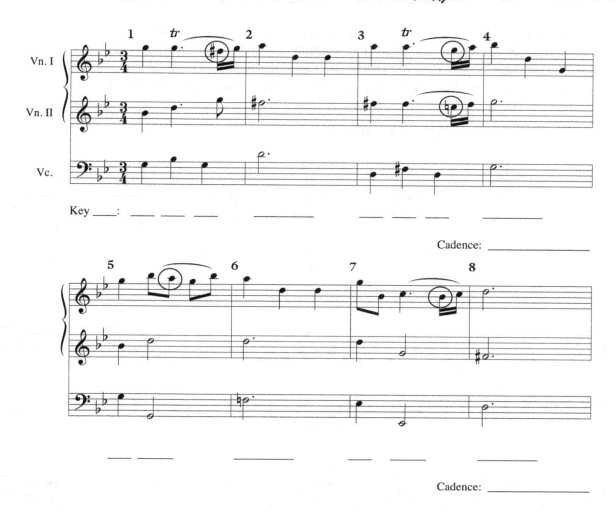

Key ____: ____ ____ ____ ____ ____ ____ ____

Cadence: _____

Cadence: _____

1F. Add the key signature and notate two chords that would create the following cadences:

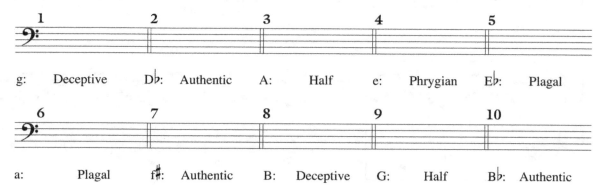

1	2	3	4	5
g: Deceptive	D♭: Authentic	A: Half	e: Phrygian	E♭: Plagal

6	7	8	9	10
a: Plagal	f♯: Authentic	B: Deceptive	G: Half	B♭: Authentic

2. HARMONIC RHYTHM

2A. Determine the key and add Roman numerals *beneath* all diatonic triads and seventh chords in the following excerpts. Add lead-sheet symbols *above* all seventh chords not diatonic in the key. Disregard chords in boxes. Show the harmonic rhythm with pitchless note values, and add bar lines that reflect this harmonic rhythm. Then, assign a probable meter.

James Pankow: "Colour My World"

2B. Barlines and meter signature have been removed from the following excerpts. Using what you've learned about harmonic rhythm, assign one of these meters to the excerpt and bar it accordingly.

1   $\frac{3}{4}$ ♩ | (Triple meter beginning on beat 3)

2   $\frac{4}{4}$ (Quadruple meter beginning on beat 1)

3   $\frac{4}{4}$ ♩ | (Quadruple meter beginning on beat 4)

4   $\frac{3}{4}$ (Triple meter beginning on beat 1)

Then list the reasons for your decision. Finally, place Roman numerals in the blanks beneath the staff and identify the cadences where asked to do so. Circled tones are nonchord tones.

1   J. S. Bach: "Was Gott tut, das ist wolhgetan" 🔊

Name cadences: _____   _____

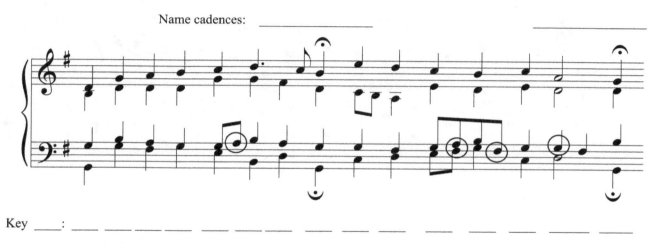

Key ___: __ __ __ __ __ __   __ __ __ __ __ __

Your reasons for choice of meter and barring:

2   Brahms: Symphony no. 1, op. 67 (fourth movement)

Name cadences: _____

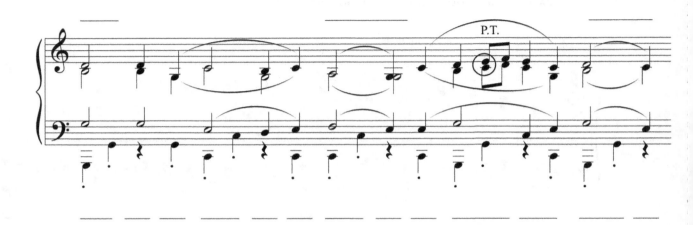

Key ____: ____ ____ ____ ____ ____ ____ ____

Your reasons for choice of meter and barring:

3 Traditional: "Old Colony Times" 🔊

Cadence: _____   Cadence: _____

Key: ___ ___ ___ ___ ___ ___ ___ ___ ___

Cadence: _____

___ ___ ___ ___ ___ ___ ___ ___ ___

Your reasons for choice of meter and barring:

4 Brahms: *Romance*, op. 18, no. 5 🔊

Key: ___   ___ ___ ___ ___ ___ ___

Your reasons for choice of meter and barring:

5   Tyler, Perry, and Rhodes: "Cryin'"

Your reasons for choice of meter and barring:

CHAPTER SEVEN

Melodic Pitch and Rhythm

1. RANGE, INTERVAL STRUCTURE, AND GESTURE

1A. For the following melodies:

1. Using the terms, ascending, descending, arch, inverted arch, or stationary, identify the general contour of each bracketed segment.

2. Describe the interval structure as prevailingly conjunct, prevailingly disjunct, or evenly balanced.

3. Write the scale on which it is based and name the tonic.

1   **Mozart: Le Nozze di Figaro, K. 492 (act 1, no. 9)**

Interval structure: _____

Scalar basis: _____

Tonic: _____

2   Chopin: Prelude op. 28, no. 6

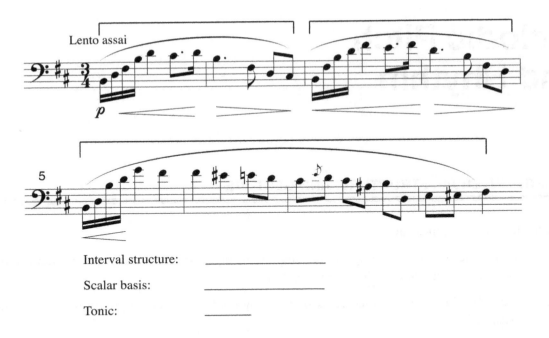

Interval structure: _____

Scalar basis: _____

Tonic: _____

3   Schumann: Traümerei (Kinderszenen, op. 15)

Interval structure: _____

Scalar basis: _____

Tonic: _____

4   Eben Rexford and Hart P. Danks: "Silver Threads Among the Gold"

Interval structure: _____

Scalar basis: _____

Tonic: _____

5   "Amazing Grace" (folk hymn)

Interval structure: _____

Scalar basis: _____

Tonic: _____

1B. Compose short melodies, as specified below.

    1   meter, 8-measure length

      Key: A major

      Contour: Arch

      Interval structure: prevailingly conjunct

    2   meter, 12-measure length

      Key: G minor

      Contour: Descending followed by ascending

      Interval structure: balanced

1C. Of the two melodies that follow:

1.   Which melody (**1** or **2**) has the wider range? ___

2.   Which melody (**1** or **2**) contains the larger leaps? ___

3.   Which melody (**1** or **2**) is more motivic? ___

4.   Which melody (**1** or **2**) contains more varied gestures? ___

5.   Which melody (**1** or **2**) rises once to a single high point? ___

1   Boccherini: *Minuet*

2   Dvorak: Symphony no. 9, op. 95 (second movement)

2. REPETITION

2A. In the two melodies from the preceding Assignment 1C, bracket all repetition, and indicate its form—exact repetition, varied repetition, or sequence.

2B. Recalling that Mozart had only three options at any point in the following composition, indicate above each measure whether it represents an exact repetition of something previous ("**R** of m. 5" for example), a variation of something previous ("**V** of m. 7" for example), or something new (**N**). Regard sequences as a type of variation. Label any of these as real or tonal.

Mozart: Piano Concerto K. 467 (first movement)

2C. Compose sequential repetitions to the melodic patterns according to the directions for each.

1   A tonal sequence of two repetitions, each a step lower, ending with a half cadence in m. 4.

2   A tonal sequence of two repetitions, each a step higher, with new melodic material in the last two measures ending with an authentic cadence.

3   A tonal sequence of two repetitions, each a step higher, with new melodic material in the last measure, ending with an authentic cadence.

4   A real sequence a major third lower at each repetition, with two final measures of new material that end with a half cadence.

2D. In the sequential passages that follow:

1. Bracket and label the first statement and each subsequent statement of the pattern.

2. Identify the sequence as real or tonal.

3. Indicate the level of transposition at each repetition.

1   **Gounod: "Ave Maria"**

2   **J. S. Bach: Brandenburg Concerto no. 2 (first movement)**

3   **Schubert: Piano Sonata D. 960 (first movement)**

4 Paul Desmond: "Take Five"

2E. In the following passages:

1. Bracket and label the first statement and each subsequent statement of the pattern.

2. Identify the sequence as real or tonal.

3. Indicate the pitch level of the transposition at each repetition.

1 Beethoven: Piano Sonata, op. 26 (second movement) 🔊

2   Brahms: Variations on a Theme by Joseph Haydn, op. 56b

3. MELODIC TONALITY

3A. In the following melodies:

1   Circle the pitches that stand out, and above each, list one or more of these reasons: a) tonal accent b) agogic accent c) high point d) low point e) beginning of a gesture f) end of a gesture

2   Identify step progressions and/or large-scale arpeggiations.

3   Identify and describe any sequences.

1   **Mozart: Piano Concerto K. 467 (second movement)**

2   Chopin: Valse op. 69, no. 2

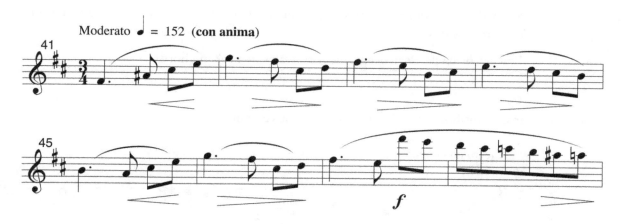

3   Schubert: Sonata in B Major, D. 575 (fourth movement)

4   Beethoven: Symphony no. 5, op. 67 (second movement)

3B. In the following melodies:

1   Show the tonic-dominant axis by placing a T (Tonic) or D (Dominant) above significant occurrences of each.

2   Bracket or circle clear occurrences of scales or broken chords.

1   **Brahms: Symphony no. 2, op. 73 (first movement)**

2   **"Scarborough Fair" (English folk song)**

3   **J. S. Bach: Cantata no. 147**

4   **Chopin: Mazurka op. 7, no. 1**

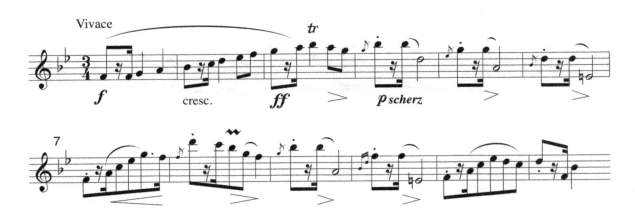

3C. Compare these two melodies in the following respects:

1   Scales and arpeggiations

2   Step progressions and large-scale arpeggiations

3   Tonic-dominant axis

4   Sequence

5   General similarity or contrast

1   **Verdi: "La Donna è Mobile (from *Rigoletto*, act 3: Canzone)**

2   **Hal Davis, Barry Gordy, Willie Hutch, and Bob West: "I'll Be There"**

3D. Identify sequences, step progressions and large-scale arpeggiations in the melodies that follow.

1   Mozart: Piano Sonata, K. 331 (third movement)

2   J.S. Bach: English Suite no. 6, BWV 811 (Gavotte II)

3   Tchaikovsky: Symphony no. 6 (first movement)

4   Beethoven: Piano Sonata op. 13 (third movement)

CHAPTER EIGHT

Embellishing Tones

1. STEP-STEP COMBINATIONS

1A. Add the embellishing tone at the specified point in a voice that can accommodate it. Change note values as necessary to maintain the correct number of beats per measure.

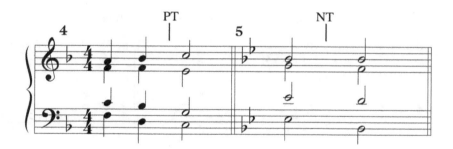

1B. Add the nonchord tone in an appropriate location and voice. Alter rhythmic values as necessary to fit the measure. For Numbers 6–10, complete the measure with the missing chord tone as well.

1C. Add either a PT or a NT in the designated voice at an appropriate point in the measure. Change note values as needed.

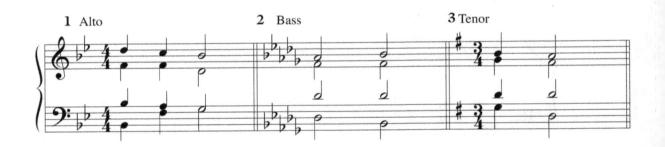

1D. Rewrite the following in the blank measures, adding a PT or NT in an appropriate voice.

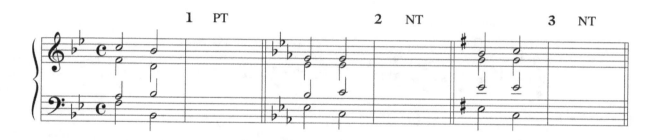

1E. Identify the PTs and NTs in the musical examples that follow. Chord symbols are given to help you identify the NCTs.

1 **Mozart: Eine Kleine Nachtmusik (third movement)**

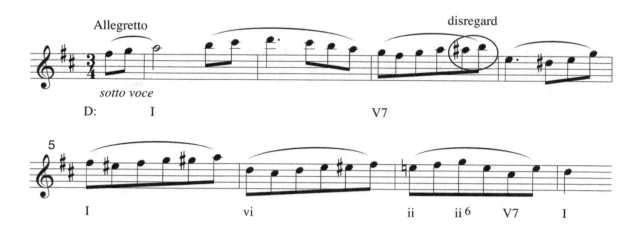

2   Traditional: "I've Been Workin' on the Railroad"

* disregard

3   Mozart: Symphony no. 40, K. 560 (first movement)

1F. Circle and label the PTs and NTS in the musical excerpts that follow. In **1**, use the given lead-sheet chord symbols to determine which tones to analyze as NCTs. In **2**, provide Roman numeral analysis based on the piano part. Label nonchord tones in the violin part, disregarding those marked with an X.

1 **Folk lullaby: "Hush Little Baby" Arr. R.T.**

2   Beethoven: Sonata for Violin and Piano, op. 24 (first movement) 🔊

F:

2. STEP-LEAP COMBINATIONS

2A. Starting on the suggested pitch, complete the empty measure with an embellishing tone, including its approach and resolution. Place the embellishing tone in an appropriate metric position.

2B. Add DNs, ETs or APPs in the appropriate voice.

2C. Circle and label all NCTs in the excerpts that follow.

1 Kuhlau: Sonatina, op. 59, no. 1 (Rondo) 🔊

2 Tchaikovsky: Piano Concerto no. 1, op. 23 (first movement) 🔊

2D. The phrases that follow are from harmonized chorales by J. S. Bach. The non-chord tones have been removed. Rewrite the music on separate manuscript paper, adding at least one PT, NT, APP, ET, and DN, distributed among the three lower voices. Then, provide Roman-numeral analysis.

1   J. S. Bach: "Auf meinen lieben Gott"

Key ____: ___ ___ ___ ___ ___ ___ ___ ___ ___

2   J. S. Bach: "Nun lob', mein Seel', den Herren"

Key ____: ___ ___ ___ ___ ___ ___ ___ ___ ___

3.   STEP-REPETITION COMBINATIONS

3A. Complete the soprano and bass lines to create the indicated suspensions. Each figure should involve two beats–one for the dissonance and one for the resolution. (The preparation is already present.)

3B. Rewrite each measure in the space provided, adding the specified nonchord tone in a voice that will accommodate it. You will have to change some of the note values to do this.

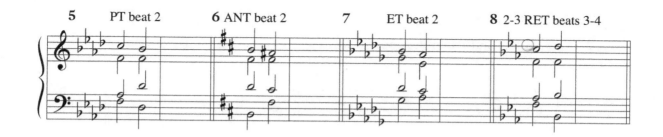

3C. In the following two-voice passages, add the specified embellishing tones in the indicated voices. To do so, you may have to change the rhythmic value of the note that immediately precedes or follows or displace a note by half a beat or a beat.

1   Add to the upper voice two PTs, an APP, and a RET.

2   Add a DN and PT in the upper voice.

3   Add a 9–8 SUS and a 4–3 SUS.

4   Add an ANT in the upper voice and a PT in the lower.

3D. Identify the embellishing tones in the musical examples that follow.

1   **Chopin: Prelude op. 28, no. 6**

2   **Beethoven: Piano Sonata op. 26 (first movement)**

3   John Rich and Scott Sax: "Like We Never Loved At All" 🔊

How can you just walk on by With out one tear in your eye? Don't you

have the slight est feel ings left for me?

4   William Royce "Boz" Scaggs: "We're All Alone" 🔊

Moderately slow

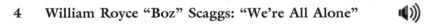

Out-side the rain be - gins, and it may nev-er end, so cry no more. On the shore a

dream will take us out to sea for - ev-er-more, for - ev-er-more

4. EMBELLISHING TONES AND STYLE

4A. The phrases that follow are from harmonized chorales by J. S. Bach. The nonchord tones have been removed. Rewrite the music on separate manuscript paper, adding the indicated nonchord tones, distributing them among the three lower voices. Then, provide Roman-numeral analysis.

1   **J. S. Bach: "Christus, der ist mein Leben"**

Add PT, ANT, 4–3 SUS, DN, AND APP

Key: ___: ___ ___ ___ ___ ___ ___ ___ ___ ___ ___

2   **J. S. Bach: "Jesu, Jesu, du bist mein"**

Add PT, 2–3 SUS, ANT, PT, AND NT

Key ___: ___ ___ ___ ___ ___ ___ ___ ___ ___ ___ ___ ___ ___ ___

4B. In the musical examples that follow:

1.   Identify all non-chord tones. In Example **1**, creating ties over the repeated melodic pitches will help you understand and identify the non-chord tones. In Example **2**, the lead-sheet symbols will tell you which notes to regard as chord members. Analyze all others as non-chord tones.

2.   Identify all sequences, step progressions, and large-scale arpeggiations if present.

1   **Ponchielli: Danza delle ore del giorno ("Dance of the Hours") from** *La Gioconda*, **act 3, scene 6** 🔊))

2   **Michael Legrand: "How Do You Keep the Music Playing?"** (from *Best Friends*)
     Arr. R.T.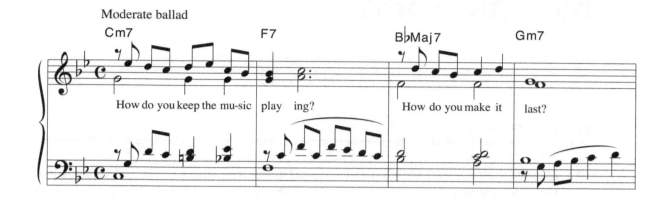

3   **J. S. Bach: "In dulci jubilo"**

CHAPTER NINE
Melodic Form

1. THE PHRASE

1A. Identify the phrases, and symbolize their relationships using the method explained on page 146. Identify sequences present and indicate the type (real or tonal). If a sentence structure is present, so indicate.

1   **Paul Gordon and Jay Gruska: "Friends and Lovers"**

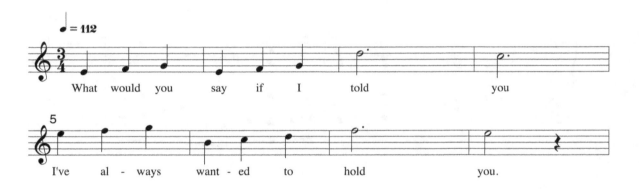

2   **Anonymous: Minuet BWV Anh. 114**

3   Larry Kusik and Nina Rota: **"Speak Softly Love"** (theme from *The Godfather*)

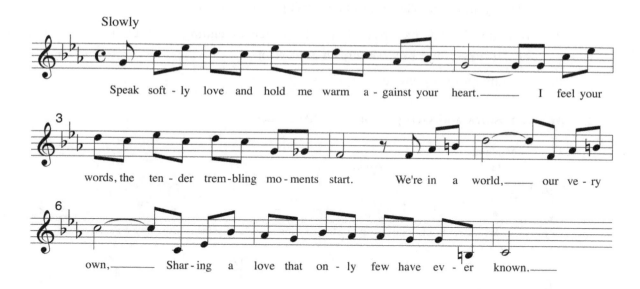

Speak soft - ly love and hold me warm a - gainst your heart._____ I feel your

words, the ten - der trem - bling mo - ments start. We're in a world,_____ our ve - ry

own,_____ Shar - ing a love that on - ly few have ev - er known._____

4   Gounod: **"Ave Maria"**

A - ve Ma - ri - a, -

Gra - ti - a ple - na, Do - mi - nus te

Vir - go se - re - na,

1B. For the following two-phrase melodies:

1. Identify and symbolize each phrase, using a, a′, b, b′ and so on.

2. Indicate the relative strength of the cadences ending each phrase—W = weaker, S = stronger—and give reasons for your answers.

3. Identify motives present.

1   **W. W. Fosdick and George Poulton: "Aura Lee"**

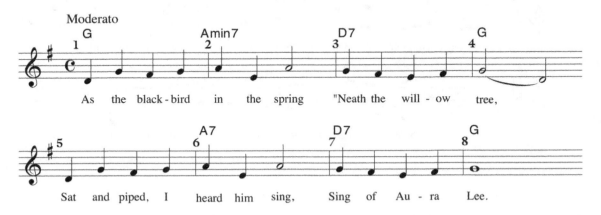

2   **Schumann: Piano Concerto, op. 54 (first movement)**

3   **Traditional (Germany)**

4   Delibes: *Coppelia* **(Prelude)**

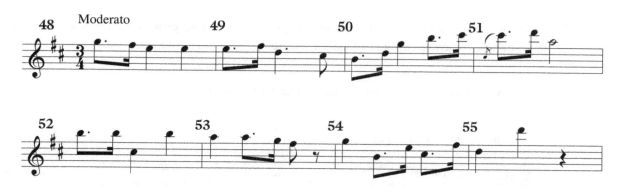

1C. To each phrase given, compose a second phrase that bears the specified relationship to the first.

more conclusive cadence

more conclusive cadence

2. COMBINING AND EXTENDING PHRASES

2A. Identify the following melodic passages as periods or phrase groups. If a period, indicate the type–parallel or contrasting. Indicate if a sentence structure is present.

1   **Beethoven: Piano sonata op. 2, no. 3 (first movement)**

2   **Mozart: Symphony K. 543 (third movement)**

3   **Mozart: Piano Sonata K. 333 (first movement)**

4 Chopin: Mazurka op. 17, no. 1

5 Percy Montross: "Clementine"

2B. 1.   Identify the melodic unit (phrase, phrase group, period, double period) formed by the
          following passages.

     2.   Identify phrase extensions as pre-cadential or post-cadential.

     3.   Identify the unifying motives.

     4.   Identify large-scale relationships such as step progressions or large-scale arpeggiations.

1   **Beethoven: String Quartet op. 18, no. 1 (first movement)**

2   Brahms: Sonata for Clarinet and Piano, op. 120 (second movement)

2C. In the following two-phrase excerpts:

    1.   Identify the unifying motive if one is present.

    2.   Tell which phrase ends more conclusively and why.

    3.   Use letters to show the relationship between the phrases.

    4.   Indicate whether the phrases form a period or a phrase group.

    5.   Identify any phrase extensions present.

    6.   For Nos. 1 and 3, circle and label NCTs.

1   **Rimsky-Korsakoff: Scheherazade (third movement)** 🔊

2   Chopin: Mazurka op. posth. 67, no. 4

3   Dutch Hymn: "Prayer of Thanksgiving" 🔊

2D. Bracket the cadential extensions in the following phrases, and indicate whether they are pre-cadential or post-cadential and whether they extend tonic or dominant harmony.

1   Haydn: Piano Sonata, K. XVI:47 (third movement)

2   Mozart: "Durch Zärtlichkeit und Schmeicheln" (from *Die Entführung aus dem Serail*, K. 384)

3   Mozart: Piano Sonata K. 282 (Menuetto I)

2E. For each given phrase, compose another bearing the indicated relationship.

1   Compose a second phrase that forms a parallel period with the first.

2   Compose a second phrase using the same metric structure as the first but forming a contrasting period.

3   Compose a contrasting phrase structured so that the two phrases form a contrasting phrase group.

2F. Provide a melodic analysis of the following excerpt:

1. Symbolize the phrase relationships and indicate whether or not a period is formed.

2. Describe the contour of each phrase.

3. Identify the unifying motive.

4. Identify all sequences.

5. Place T or D above prominent tonic and dominant pitches.

6. Identify the high point.

7. Identify any step progressions or large-scale arpeggiations.

Chopin: Prelude op. 28, no. 7

Haydn: "Gennzinger" Sonata (first movement) 🔊

2G. Complete the following assignment in as musical a way as you can.

1 Add a consequent phrase that creates a parallel period. Make the phrase the same length as the antecedent and incorporate some of the same rhythms.

Begin here

2 Add a consequent phrase whose first gesture is based on m. 3 of the antecedent (contour and rhythm, but not necessarily the pitches). Then develop the phrase so that it forms a contrasting period.

3 Precede the given phrase with one related in such a way that the two form a phrase group symbolized a a'.

4   Add two phrases to the given two to form a double period: a b a′ c. Compose phrase c to resemble phrase b, but extend it by two or four measures prior to the cadence (a precadential extension).

(Compose a phrase extension here.)

CHAPTER TEN

Melodic Principles of Part Writing

The Outer-Voice Framework

1. MELODIC PRINCIPLES

1A. Name the key. Then, circle and explain departures from the melodic principles presented in the first section of this chapter.

1   Key: _____

(for soprano)

2   Key: _____

(for alto)

3   Key: _____

(for tenor)

4   Key: ___

1B. 1.   Refer back to the six melodic principles listed on page 168. Which did Bach observe in the following excerpts? Circle the relevant pitches and identify the principle involved.

2.   In the blanks, identify the type of motion (P = Parallel; S = Similar; O = Oblique; C = Contrary) between the soprano and bass.

1   J. S. Bach: "Ach, dass nicht die lezte Stunde"

Motion: _ _ _ _ _ _ _ _ _ _ _ _ _ _ _ _ _ _

2   J. S. Bach: "Brunnquell aller Güter"

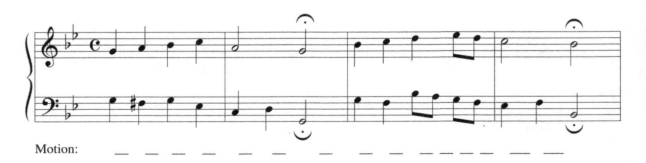

Motion: _ _ _ _ _ _ _ _ _ _ _

1C. In the blanks, identify the interval formed by the two voices. Then, create the requested type
of melodic motion (P = Parallel; S = Similar; O = Oblique; C = Contrary) by moving the
incomplete voice to a note that forms a *consonance* with the other voice. (If you've forgotten
which intervals are consonances, refer to page 30.)

1D. In the following chorale harmonization:

    1.   Show the range of each voice part.

    2.   For each voice, indicate the number of times a leap larger than a third occurs.

    3.   Indicate which voice contains the largest leaps.

    4.   Identify the most disjunct voice overall.

J.S. Bach: "Du Friedensfürst, Herr Jesu Christ"

Range: S _____   A _____   T _____   B _____

Leaps larger than a third: _____   _____   _____   _____

Voice with largest leaps: _____

Most disjunct voice: _____

1E. In the blanks beneath the music, indicate the type of motion (Contrary, Oblique, Similar, Parallel) between the soprano and bass. Then, tell how many times each mention occurs.

J.S. Bach: "Ach Gott, wie manches Herzelied"

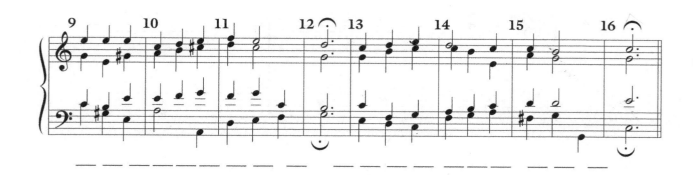

2. CREATING AN OUTER-VOICE FRAMEWORK

2A. Add a soprano to the given bass to create 1:1 counterpoint. Use only consonances and strive for as much contrary or oblique motion as possible.

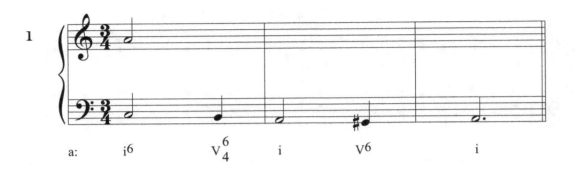

1

a: i⁶   V$^6_4$ i   V⁶   i

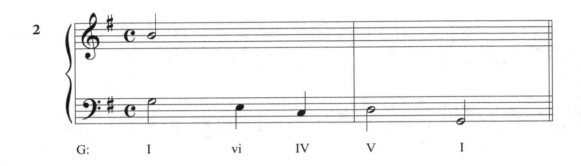

2

G: I   vi   IV   V   I

3

d: i   i   V⁶   i   VII⁶   III   ii°⁶   V   i   VI   iv   V   i

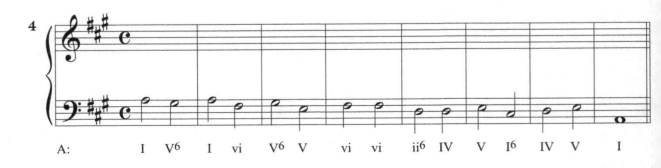

4

A: I   V⁶   I   vi   V⁶   V   vi   vi   ii⁶   IV   V   I⁶   IV   V   I

2B. Add a soprano to Bach's bass lines to create 1:1 counterpoint consisting entirely of consonances. (Do not add a separate note against the circled nonchord tones.) After doing so, insert embellishing tones or additional chord tones in either the soprano or bass to create occasional 2:1 counterpoint.

1   J.S. Bach: "Kommt her zu mir, spricht Gottes Sohn"

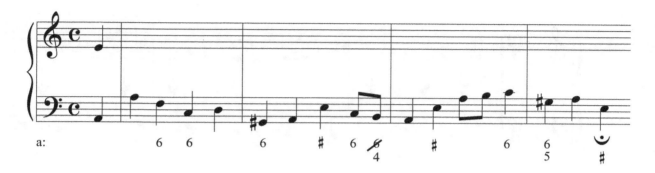

2   J.S. Bach: "Was Gott tut, das ist wohlgetan"

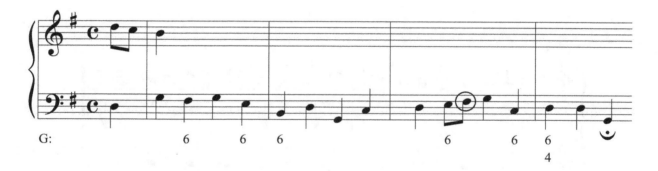

2C. On the blank staff, re-notate the bass line, creating 2:1 counterpoint at the locations marked by arrows. Remember that you can accomplish this by adding PTs, NTs or additional chord tones. Remember also that NCTs can be added not only between beats but also *on* the beats by shifting the position of an existing note.

Frank Loesser and Hoagy Carmichael: "Heart and Soul"

2D. Embellish the soprano to create a prevailing 2:1 counterpoint. Any and all NCTs are available to you as well as additional chord tones. Feel free to displace the given soprano pitches where doing so will improve the counterpoint or the melodic line itself.

G: I V⁶ vi I⁶₄ ii⁶ vi V V⁴₂ I⁶ iii IV vi ii⁶ V I

CHAPTER ELEVEN

The Melodic Factor in Four-Voice Part Writing

Voicing and Connecting Chords

1. VOICING CHORDS

1A. Provide Roman-numeral symbols (including superscripts to show inversions) in the blanks. Then, place an X above the chords not doubled according to the procedures explained in this chapter.

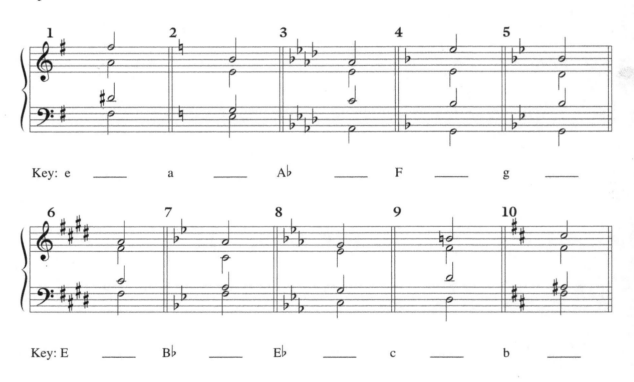

Key: e ____   a ____   A♭ ____   F ____   g ____

Key: E ____   B♭ ____   E♭ ____   c ____   b ____

1B. Improve the spacing where needed. Do this without changing the soprano and bass or the doubling. Keep each voice within its range and maintain normal disposition–soprano above alto, alto above tenor, and tenor above bass. Indicate chords not requiring re-spacing with the notation "O.K."

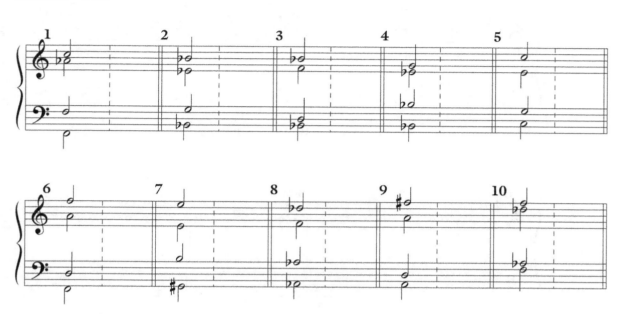

1C. Provide Roman-numeral symbols (including superscripts to show inversions) in the blanks. Then, retaining the same doubling and without changing the soprano or bass notes, provide a second acceptable voicing for each chord.

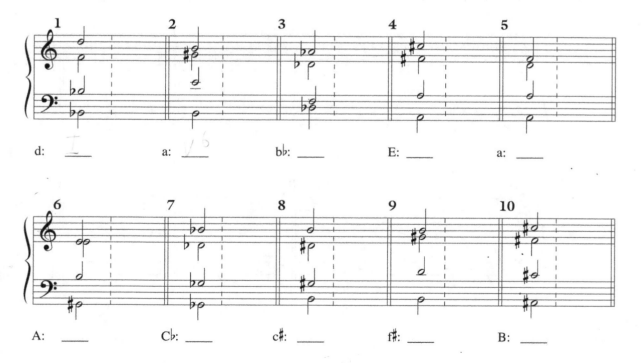

1D. Voice the chords, using appropriate spacing and the doubling preferences given on pages 181–183.

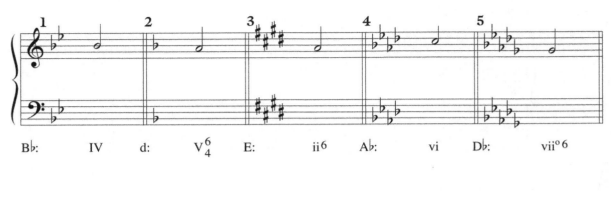

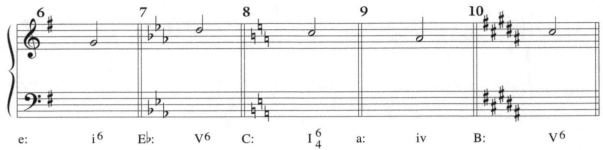

1E. Voice the chords indicated by the figured bass, using appropriate doubling and spacing.

1F. Provide Roman numerals. Then indicate whether the soprano (S) or bass (B) is doubled, which chord member (R, 3, or 5) is doubled, and which scale degree (1, 4, 5 and so on) is doubled. A suspension is present. Locate it and identify the type.

J. S. Bach: "Ermuntre dich, mein schwacher Geist" 🔊

Key G: <u>V</u> __ __ __ __ __ __ __ __ __ __ __

Voice doubled: <u>B</u> __ __ __ __ __ __ __ __ __ __

Chord member doubled: <u>R</u> __ __ __ __ __ __ __ __ __ __

Scale degree doubled: <u>5</u> __ __ __ __ __ __ __ __ __ __

2. CONNECTING CHORDS

2A. Identify the voice-leading errors in the following three-chord successions. (More than a single error may exist.) Provide harmonic analysis.

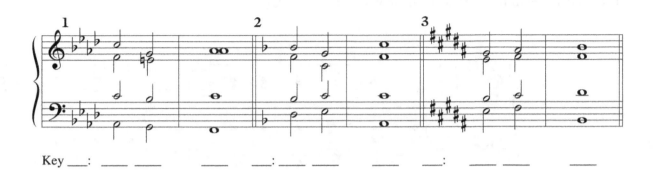

Key ___: ___ ___ ___   ___: ___ ___   ___: ___ ___ ___

___: ___ ___ ___   ___: ___ ___   ___: ___ ___ ___   ___: ___ ___ ___

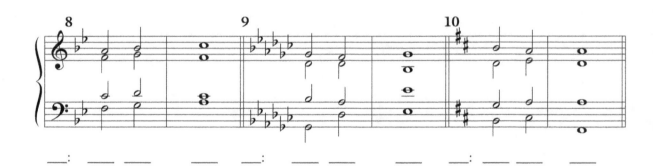

___: ___ ___ ___   ___: ___ ___   ___: ___ ___ ___

2B. Identify the voice-leading errors in the following four-part passage. Possible errors are:

(a) too large a melodic leap

(b) too many leaps in a row (exclude the bass)

(c) non-resolution of a sensitive tone

(d) spacing

(e) doubling

(f) consecutive fifths or octaves

(g) voice crossing

(h) voice overlap

Numbers indicate the location of problems.

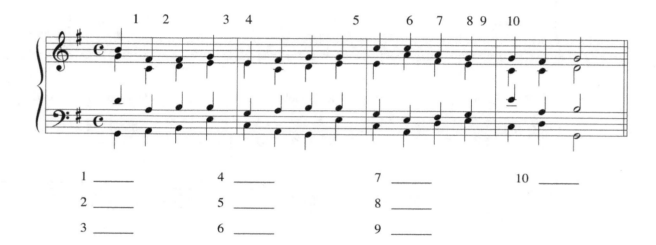

1 _____	4 _____	7 _____	10 _____
2 _____	5 _____	8 _____
3 _____	6 _____	9 _____

2C. Correct the indicated voice-leading problems. In doing so, change neither the chords nor the soprano and bass—unless the problem exists in the soprano or bass.

2D. Some of the following two-chord successions contain common tones. Part write each succession, retaining common tones if present. If common tones are not present, move the upper voices in similar motion contrary to the bass. Resolve sensitive tones.

d: VI   iv   c: V   i   e: iv   i   Bb: iii   vi   E: V   vi

Gb: IV   V   d: V   i   a: ii°6   V   Eb: ii6   V   A: IV   V

2E. Part write in four voices the following two-chord successions using the appropriate doubling, spacing, and chord connection procedures.

2F. Add the key signature, and illustrate in four voices the cadences. Provide harmonic analysis.

1 Plagal   **2** Perfect Authentic   **3** Half

g: _____ _____   c#: _____ _____   E: _____ _____

4 Deceptive   **5** Phrygian half   **6** Imperfect Authentic

Db: _____ _____   b: _____ _____   Ab: _____ _____

CHAPTER TWELVE

Part Writing with Root-Position Triads

The Chorale

1. PART WRITING WITH ROOT-POSITION TRIADS

1A. Connect the following root-position triads. Retain the common tone where possible. Otherwise, move the upper voices contrary to the bass. Provide lead-sheet symbols in the blanks above the chords.

1B. Connect the root-position triads. In minor keys, alter the V so that it is a major triad. In Nos. 1–5, retain the common tone in the same voice. In Nos. 6–10, do not retain the common tone, but rather, move the three upper voices in contrary motion to the bass. Provide Roman numerals.

1C. Connect the following root-position triads. Retain both common tones where possible. Where this is not possible, move all voices to a different note. Provide Roman numeral analysis.

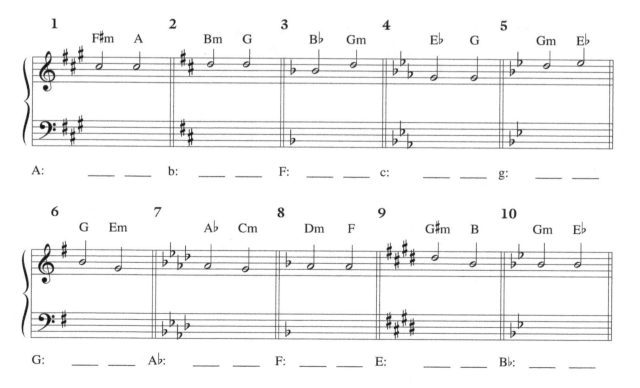

1D. Connect the root-position triads. Retain common tones when present between chords.
Otherwise, move the three upper voices contrary to the bass, if possible. In number 5, the first
chord has already been voiced, using a less common doubling in order to avoid the augmented
second that can occur between VI and V in minor keys. Provide harmonic analysis.

1E. Connect the following root-position triads. Move the upper voices contrary to the bass where possible. Provide lead-sheet symbols in the blanks above the chords.

B♭: IV V D♭: V vi B: ii iii G: IV V E: iii IV

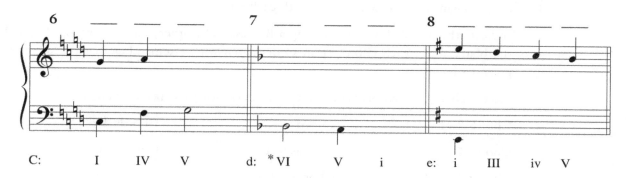

C: I IV V   d: *VI V i   e: i III iv V

* use doubling similar to that used in the deceptive cadence

1F. Part write the following deceptive cadences, observing the voice-leading principles given on pages 198–199.

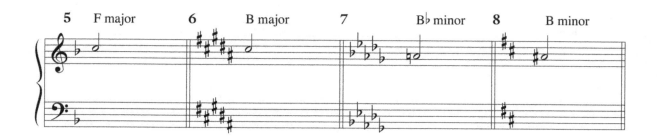

1G. Identify the part-writing errors in the following passage.

1H. In the passage that follows:

1. Add Roman-numeral symbols beneath each chord.

2. Indicate the doubled note by placing a B (Bass), O (Other), or X (Nothing doubled) in the blank above each chord. If an O or X, tell why. (Remember that the melody was given to Bach.)

3. Place a check in each blank where the common tone has been retained:

Chords 1–2 ___   Chords 2–3 ___   Chords 4–5 ___

Chords 7–8 ___   Chords 9–10 ___   Chords 10–11 ___

Chords 12–13 ___   Chords 13–14 ___

4. What part-writing procedure is employed for those points where the common tone is not retained? (Refer to the guidelines on pages 195–196.)

J.S. Bach: "Du Friedensfürst, Herr Jesu Christ" 🔊

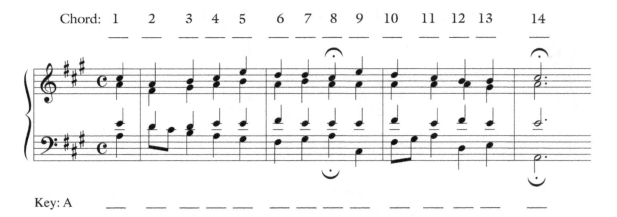

II. Part write the following passages for SATB, observing all guidelines for chord connection.

2. PART WRITING SUSPENSIONS

2A.   Rewrite each of the following to incorporate a suspension or retardation. The only voice that should change is the one containing the nonchord tone.

2B.   Part write the two-chord successions, voicing the chords so that the suspension appears in the indicated voice.

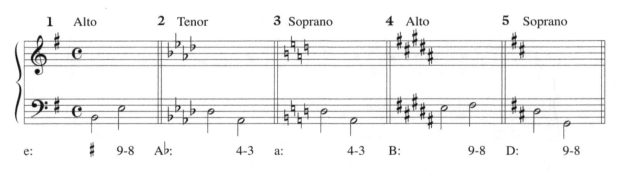

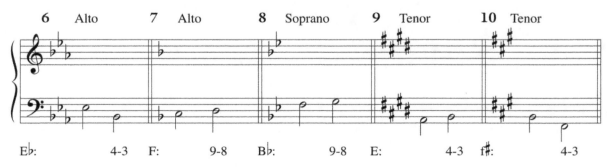

2C. Complete the passages in four voices. As in figured bass notation, hyphenated superscript combinations indicate suspensions.

1

Bb: I   V   vi 4-3 Eb: IV   V 9-8 I 9-8

2

3

G: I   V 4-3 vi 9-8 V I f#: i   iv   V 4-#3 i

4

5

d: iv V4-#3 i   a: i   VI   iv V4-#3

6

2D. Part write for SATB and add the indicated nonchord tone.

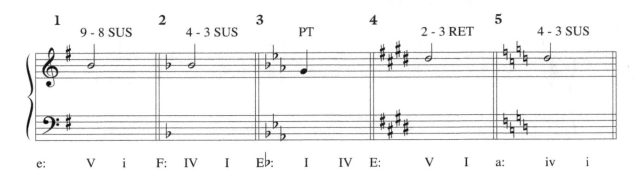

e: V   i   F: IV   I   Eb: I   IV   E: V   I   a: iv   i

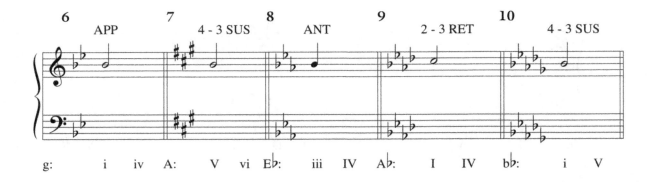

g: i   iv   A: V   vi   Eb: iii   IV   Ab: I   IV   bb: i   V

2E. The nonchord tones have been replaced by symbols at their locations. Provide harmonic analysis and add the nonchord tones. (To add suspensions, it will be necessary to alter the existing note values.)

J.S. Bach: "Nun lob', mein Seel', den Herren" 🔊

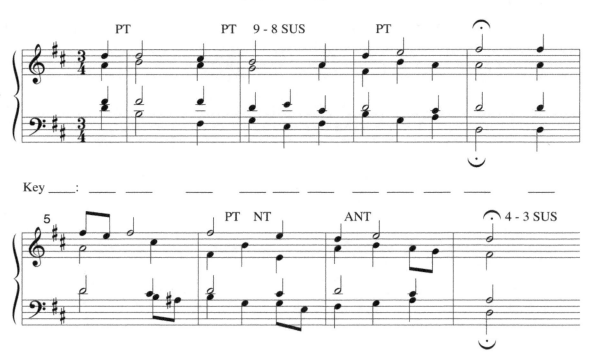

Key ___: ___   ___   ___   ___   ___   ___   ___

___   ___   ___   ___

2F. Circle and label all NCTs in the following passages. For each suspension, indicate the type. Then, provide lead-sheet chord symbols in the blanks. Disregard the music enclosed in the box.

1   J.S. Bach: "Freu' dich sehr, o meine Seele"

2   J.S. Bach: "Wo Gott zum Haus nicht gibt"

2G. Complete the passages in four voices. The single numbers between chords indicate passing tones. The hyphenated combinations indicate suspensions or retardations.

1

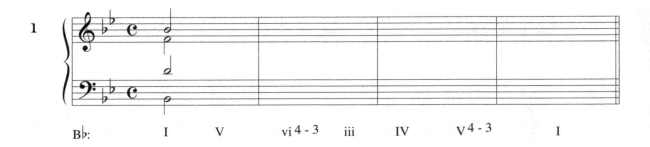

B♭:   I   V   vi 4 - 3   iii   IV   V 4 - 3   I

2

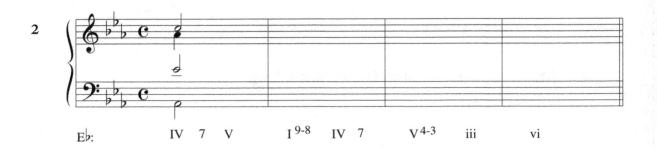

E♭:   IV 7   V   I 9-8   IV 7   V 4-3   iii   vi

3   Refer back to page 182 regarding doubling of the diminished triad.

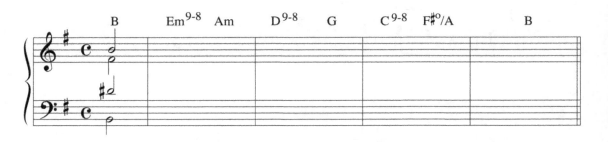

B   Em 9-8   Am   D 9-8   G   C 9-8   F#°/A   B

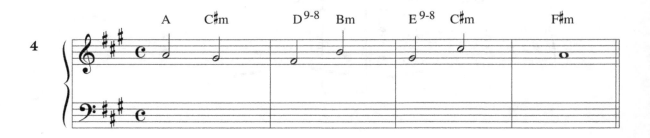

A   C#m   D 9-8   Bm   E 9-8   C#m   F#m

4

CHAPTER THIRTEEN

Part Writing with Triads in Inversion

1.   FIRST INVERSION

1A.   Improve or add the bass line as instructed.

1.   Rewrite the bass, making it more stepwise by adding passing tones and changing three chords to first inversion. Be sure your improvements don't result in a doubled leading tone.

"Good King Wenceslas" (traditional)

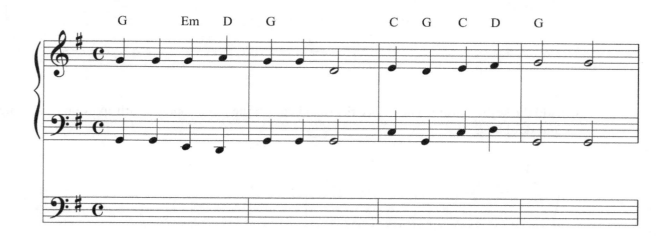

2. Add a bass line to the melody. Use the given chords, but invert to make the bass line is as stepwise as possible. Then provide a Roman-numeral description of the implied harmonies.

Dennis Lambert and Brian Potter: "One Tin Soldier" (from *Billy Jack*)

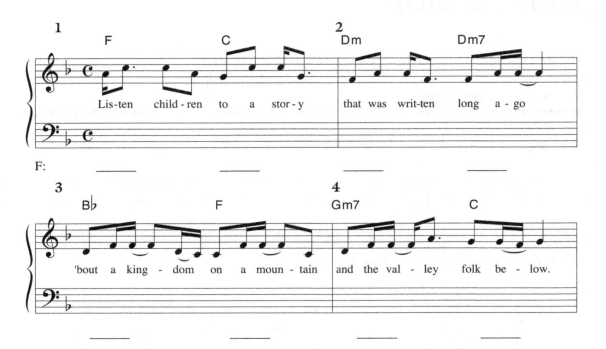

1B. Add the key signature. Then voice the triad beneath the given soprano with appropriate spacing and doubling.

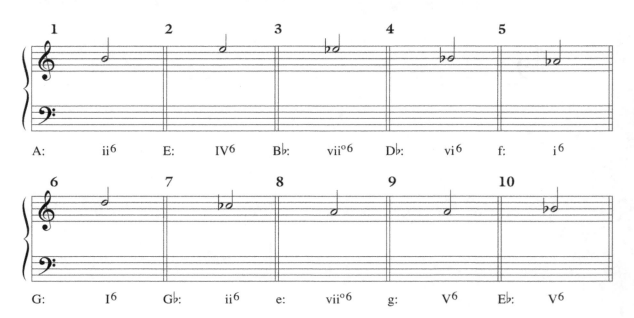

1C. Part write in four voices the two-chord successions, using appropriate doubling, spacing, and chord-connection procedures.

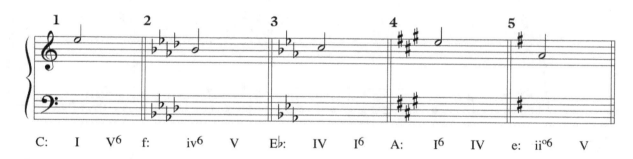

C: I   V⁶   f: iv⁶   V   Eb: IV   I⁶   A: I⁶   IV   e: ii°⁶   V

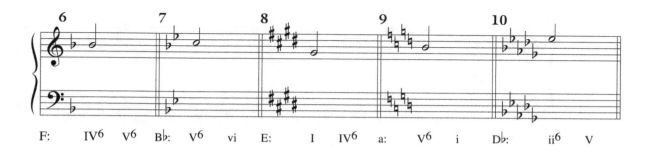

F: IV⁶   V⁶   Bb: V⁶   vi   E: I   IV⁶   a: V⁶   i   Db: ii⁶   V

1D. Add soprano, alto, and tenor voices to the figured-bass lines. Then provide harmonic analysis.

1E.   Using the framework provided, add alto and tenor voices.

J. S. Bach: "Gott lebet noch"

F: I⁶   I   IV   I⁶   ii   V⁶   I   V

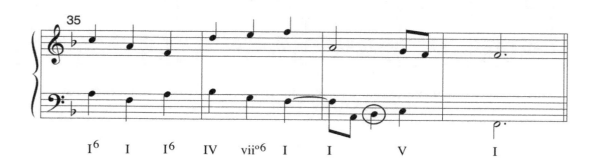

I⁶   I   I⁶   IV   vii°⁶   I   I   V   I

1F.   Realize the figured bass line, adding soprano, alto, and tenor. Provide harmonic analysis.

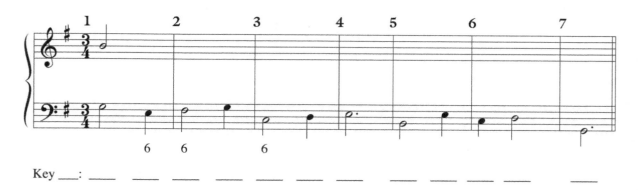

Key ___: ___   ___   ___   ___   ___   ___   ___   ___   ___   ___

1G. Part write the two-chord successions. Remember that the final number in a suspension figure suggests the inversion of the chord at resolution.

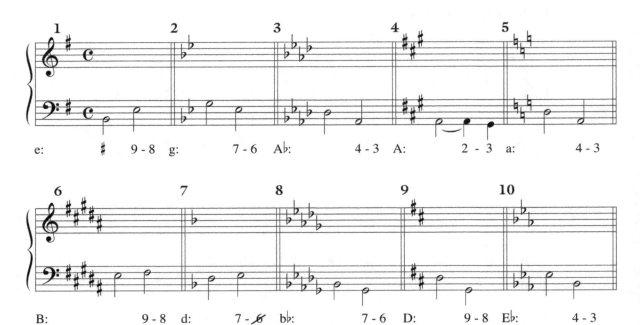

1H. Complete the following suspensions and retardations for four voices. Each figure should involve two beats—one for the dissonance and one for the resolution. Provide harmonic analysis where needed.

II.   Realize the following figured bass lines. Then provide Roman-numeral analysis.

Key ___: ___ ___ ___ ___ ___ ___ ___

Key ___: ___ ___ ___ ___ ___ ___ ___ ___

1J. Add lead-sheet symbols above the following arrangement. On separate manuscript paper, renotate the passage, creating six 9–8 suspensions in the inner voices. (Remember that a suspension can only be added to a voice when it descends by step.)

Oscar Hammerstein and Jerome Kern: "All the Things You Are" (from *Very Warm for May*) **Arr. R.T.**

2. SECOND INVERSION

2A. For the following excerpts:

1. Provide Roman numerals or lead-sheet symbols.

2. Identify the six-four chord used.

1   **Mozart: Piano Sonata K. 331 (second movement)** 🔊

Key: _____   _____   _____   _____

2   **Beethoven: Piano Sonata op. 26 (third movement)** 🔊

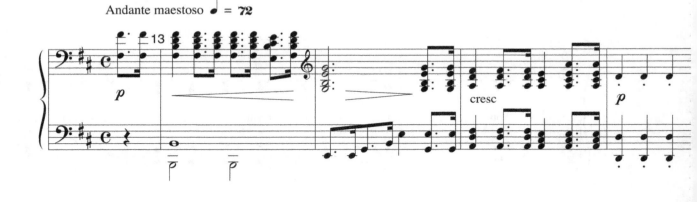

Key: D   _____   _____   _____   _____

3   Beethoven: Piano Sonata op. 2, no. 3 (third movement)

Key a: ____

4   Paul Simon: "Bridge Over Troubled Water"

Lead-Sheet Symbols: ____

2B.   Realize the following figured bass passages and identify the type of six-four chord. Provide harmonic analysis.

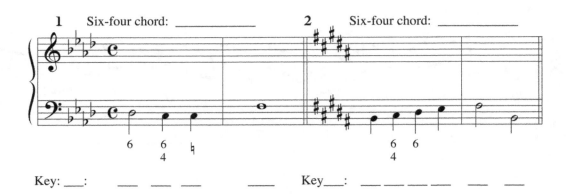

1   Six-four chord: _____

2   Six-four chord: _____

Key: ___: __ __ __   __

Key___: __ __ __ __   __

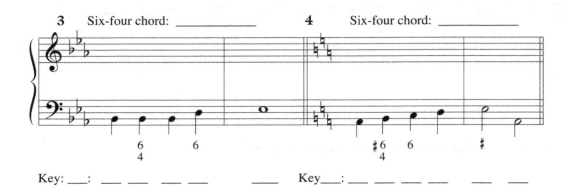

3   Six-four chord: _____

4   Six-four chord: _____

Key: ___: __ __ __ __   __

Key___: __ __ __ __   __

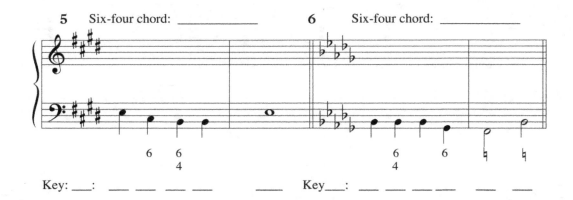

5   Six-four chord: _____

6   Six-four chord: _____

Key: ___: __ __ __   __

Key___: __ __ __ __ __

2C. Add the three missing voices to the following passages, choosing a cadential, passing, or pedal six-four chord at the point indicated. Then provide a harmonic analysis. (The bass lines are unfigured.)

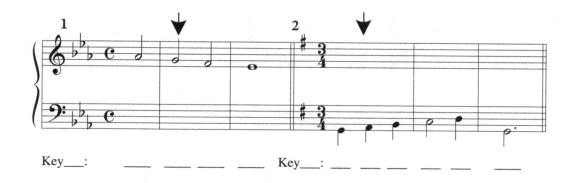

Key___: ___ ___ ___ ___   Key___: ___ ___ ___ ___ ___

Key d: ___ ___ ___ ___ ___ ___   Key G♭: ___ ___ ___ ___ ___

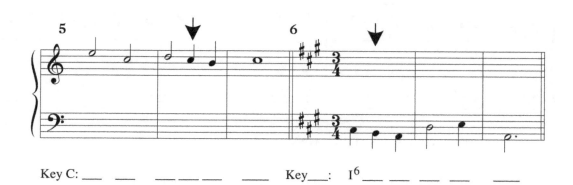

Key C: ___ ___ ___ ___ ___ ___   Key___: I⁶ ___ ___ ___ ___ ___

2D. Identify the type of six-four chord in each phrase. Indicate with an X those not properly part written, and describe the errors.

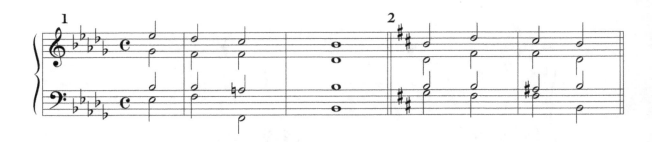

2E. Add alto, tenor, and bass.

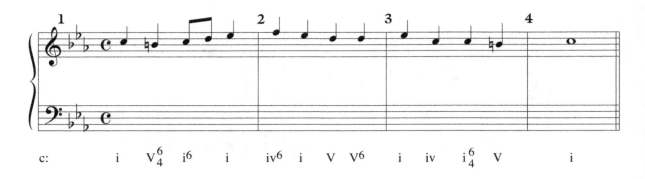

c: i   V$_4^6$ i^6 i   iv^6 i   V   V^6 i   iv   i$_4^6$ V   i

2F. Provide a harmonic analysis of the chorale fragment. Circle and label all nonchord tones. Identify six-four chords by type.

J. S. Bach: "Jesu, Jesu, du bist mein"

Key: E♭

2G. Add alto and tenor to the following, and provide harmonic analysis. Identify all six-four chords as passing, cadential, pedal, or arpeggiated. A "7" between beats indicates a passing seventh.

Key ___ : ___ ___ ___ ___ ___ ___ ___ ___ ___ ___ ___ ___

Key ___ : ___ ___ ___ ___ ___ ___ ___ ___ ___ ___ ___ ___

CHAPTER FOURTEEN

Part Writing Seventh Chords

1. DOMINANT-FUNCTIONING SEVENTH CHORDS

1A. Beneath each chord, indicate the key in which it functions as a V7. Place an X beneath any chord that is *not* a dominant seventh chord.

Key: ____ ____ ____ ____ ____ ____ ____ ____ ____ ____

1B. Supply the key and Roman numeral symbol. Then resolve the following root-position seventh chords to root-position tonic triads. Be sure to resolve the leading tone and the chord seventh.

Key ___: ___ ___ ___: ___ ___ ___: ___ ___ ___: ___ ___ ___: ___ ___

Key ___: ___ ___ ___ ___: ___ ___ ___: ___ ___ ___: ___ ___ ___: ___ ___

1C. Beneath the given soprano pitch, construct in four voices a dominant seventh chord in the key and inversion indicated (R = root position, 1 = first inversion, 2 = second inversion, 3 = third inversion). Observe correct spacing, and do not omit any chord tones.

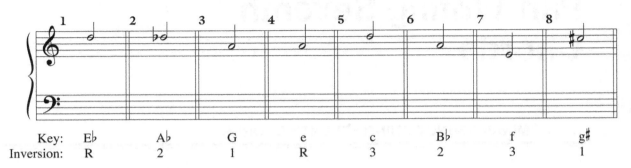

Key:	Eb	Ab	G	e	c	Bb	f	g#
Inversion:	R	2	1	R	3	2	3	1

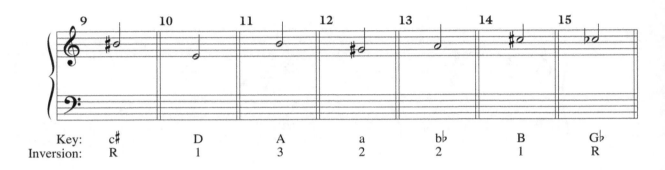

Key:	c#	D	A	a	bb	B	Gb
Inversion:	R	1	3	2	2	1	R

1D. Resolve the following figured-bass patterns. Then provide Roman numeral analysis.

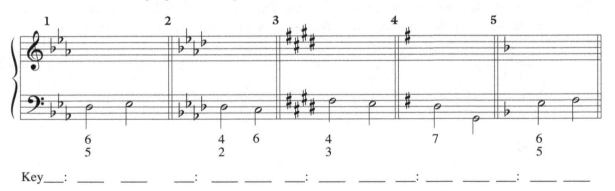

Key___: ___ ___ ___: ___ ___ ___: ___ ___ ___: ___ ___ ___: ___ ___

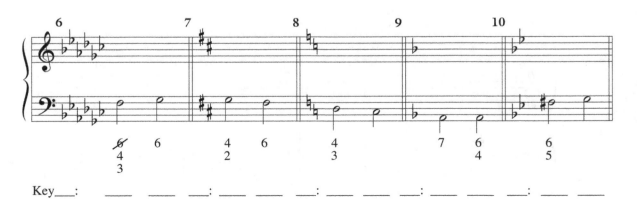

Key___: ___ ___ ___: ___ ___ ___: ___ ___ ___: ___ ___ ___: ___ ___

1E. Resolve each dominant seventh chord to a root-position or first-inversion tonic–whichever is more appropriate. Provide harmonic analysis, making sure that the superscripts reflect the inversions.

Eb: _____ _____   bb: _____ _____   e: _____ _____   c#: _____ _____   d: _____ _____

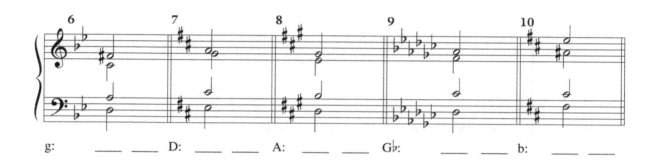

g: _____ _____   D: _____ _____   A: _____ _____   Gb: _____ _____   b: _____ _____

1F. Realize the figured-bass lines for four voices. Provide harmonic analysis.

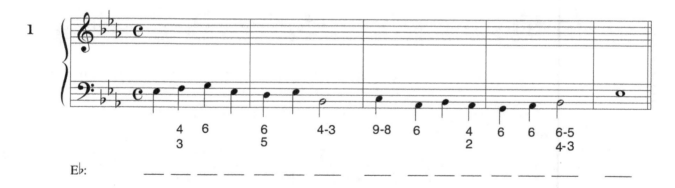

Eb: _____ _____ _____ _____ _____ _____ _____ _____ _____ _____ _____

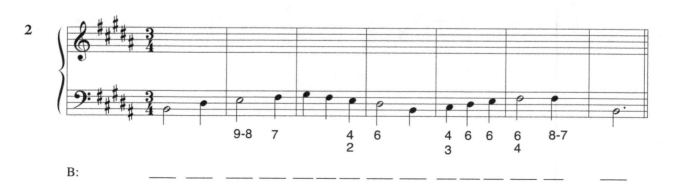

B: _____ _____ _____ _____ _____ _____ _____ _____ _____

1G.   Identify the following dominant seventh and leading-tone seventh chords by Roman numeral and superscript (to show inversion).

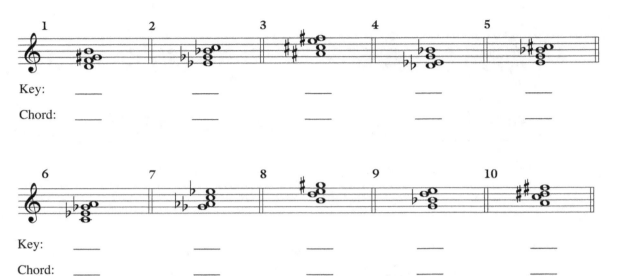

Key: ____   ____   ____   ____   ____

Chord: ____   ____   ____   ____   ____

Key: ____   ____   ____   ____   ____

Chord: ____   ____   ____   ____   ____

1H.   Resolve the leading tone seventh chords. Provide harmonic analysis.

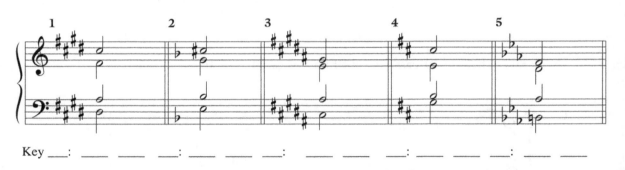

Key ___: ____ ____ ____: ____ ____ ___: ____ ____ ___: ____ ____ ___: ____ ____

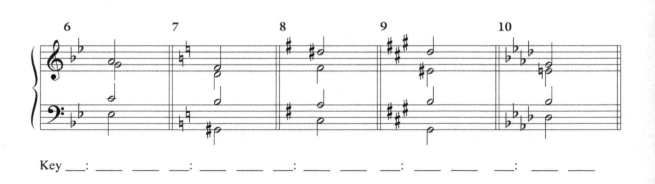

Key ___: ____ ____ ____: ____ ____ ___: ____ ____ ___: ____ ____ ___: ____ ____

II. Retaining the voicing of the first chord, resolve it, eliminating the part-writing errors present. Provide harmonic analysis.

1J.   Provide harmonic analysis of the excerpts that follow. Circle and label all nonchord tones. Indicate inversions of all chords. Draw a line to connect chord sevenths with their resolutions. Identify the types of six-four chord present in **2** and **3**.

Note: **3** also contains a major-key viio7.

1   J. S. Bach: "O Herzensangst" 🔊

Eb:

2   Mozart: Rondo, K. 485 🔊

D:

3   Brahms: Ballade op. 10, no. 4

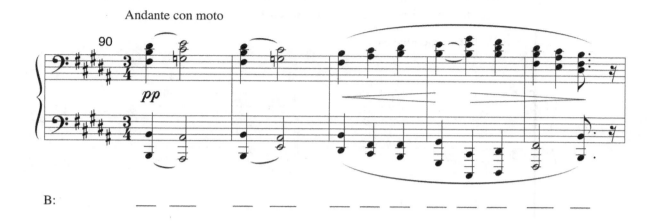

B: ___ ___ ___ ___ ___ ___ ___

2.   NONDOMINANT SEVENTH CHORDS

2A. Add the root-position seventh chord whose root lies a fifth above the root of the given chord. As a first step, place the seventh of the chord in a voice that permits its stepwise downward resolution. Provide harmonic analysis.

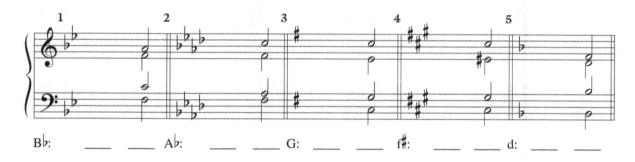

B♭: ___ ___   A♭: ___ ___   G: ___ ___   f♯: ___ ___   d: ___ ___

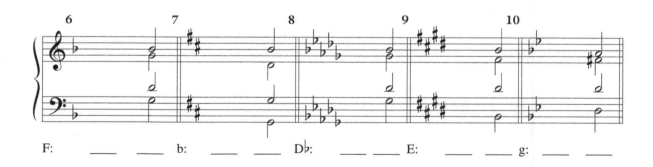

F: ___ ___   b: ___ ___   D♭: ___ ___   E: ___ ___   g: ___ ___

2B. 1.   On the extra blank staff, stack the seventh chord in root position.

2.   Resolve each chord in the most common manner. A prime consideration should be the stepwise downward resolution of the seventh.

3.   Provide harmonic analysis.

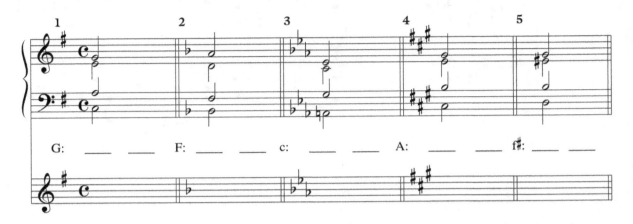

G: ___ ___   F: ___ ___   c: ___ ___   A: ___ ___   f#: ___ ___

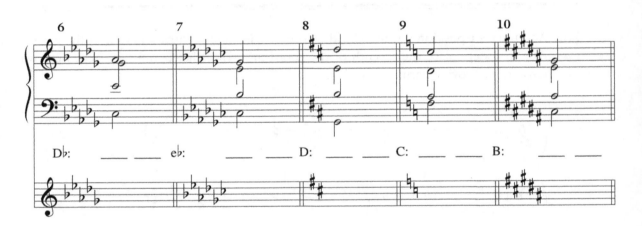

Db: ___ ___   eb: ___ ___   D: ___ ___   C: ___ ___   B: ___ ___

2C. Seventh chords in succession are indicated in the following figured bass lines. Part write for SATB, and use incomplete seventh chords only where necessary. An initial voicing is suggested. Remember that a repeated chord presents an opportunity to change voicing.

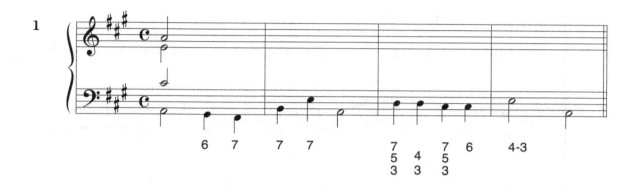

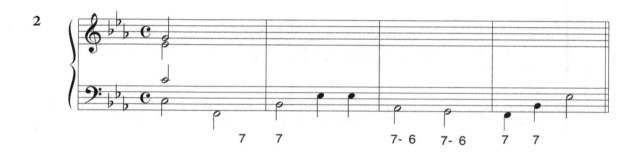

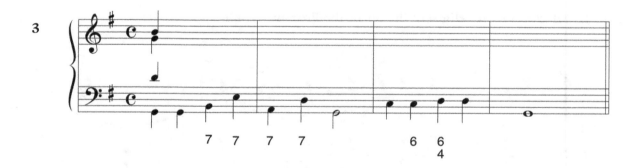

2D. In the melody with *unfigured* bass that follows:

1.   Identify the cadences.

2.   Symbolize the phrase structure.

3.   Identify all sequences.

Using appropriate harmonies, add alto and tenor voices. Use seventh chords where possible.

2E. Provide harmonic analysis. In each seventh chord, the seventh could be analyzed as a type of nonchord tone. Indicate the type.

1   **J.S. Bach: "O wie selig seid ihr doch, ihr Frommen"**

F:

2 J.S.Bach: "Werde munter, mein Gemüte"

Bb: _ _ _ _ _ _ _ _ _ _

2F. Above each seventh chord, indicate the nature of the seventh (suspension, passing tone, and so on). Draw an arrow to its resolution.

J. S. Bach: Prelude no. 1 from *Das Wohltemperierte Clavier*, vol. I

CHAPTER FIFTEEN
Secondary Function I

1. SECONDARY DOMINANTS

1A. Provide the Roman numeral symbol for these secondary dominants.

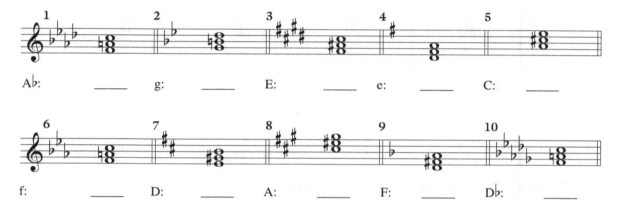

Ab: _____   g: _____   E: _____   e: _____   C: _____

f: _____   D: _____   A: _____   F: _____   Db: _____

1B. Add the key signature and construct the following chords for SATB, using appropriate doubling and spacing.

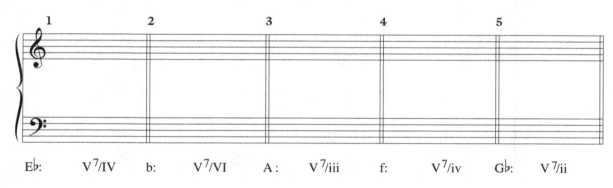

Eb: V^7/IV   b: V^7/VI   A: V^7/iii   f: V^7/iv   Gb: V^7/ii

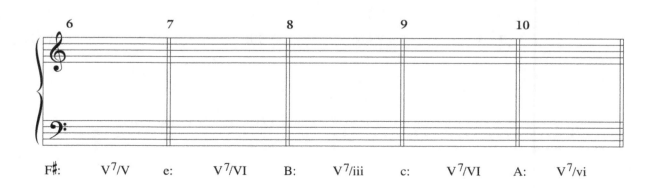

F#: V^7/V   e: V^7/VI   B: V^7/iii   c: V^7/VI   A: V^7/vi

1C. Give the Roman numeral symbol (with superscript) that represents each chord's function in the indicated keys.

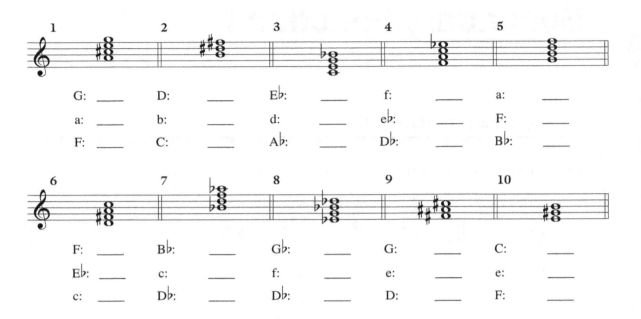

	1	2	3	4	5
	G: ____	D: ____	Eb: ____	f: ____	a: ____
	a: ____	b: ____	d: ____	eb: ____	F: ____
	F: ____	C: ____	Ab: ____	Db: ____	Bb: ____

	6	7	8	9	10
	F: ____	Bb: ____	Gb: ____	G: ____	C: ____
	Eb: ____	c: ____	f: ____	e: ____	e: ____
	c: ____	Db: ____	Db: ____	D: ____	F: ____

1D. Name the key in which each chord functions as shown.

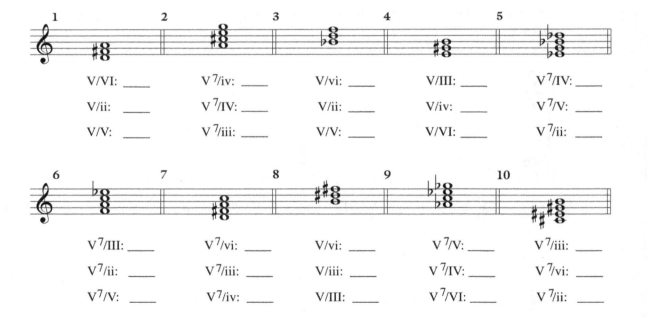

	1	2	3	4	5
	V/VI: ____	V⁷/iv: ____	V/vi: ____	V/III: ____	V⁷/IV: ____
	V/ii: ____	V⁷/IV: ____	V/ii: ____	V/iv: ____	V⁷/V: ____
	V/V: ____	V⁷/iii: ____	V/V: ____	V/VI: ____	V⁷/ii: ____

	6	7	8	9	10
	V⁷/III: ____	V⁷/vi: ____	V/vi: ____	V⁷/V: ____	V⁷/iii: ____
	V⁷/ii: ____	V⁷/iii: ____	V/iii: ____	V⁷/IV: ____	V⁷/vi: ____
	V⁷/V: ____	V⁷/iv: ____	V/III: ____	V⁷/VI: ____	V⁷/ii: ____

1E. Add the key signature, then show the figured bass that indicates the chord and inversion. Include accidentals in the figures where needed.

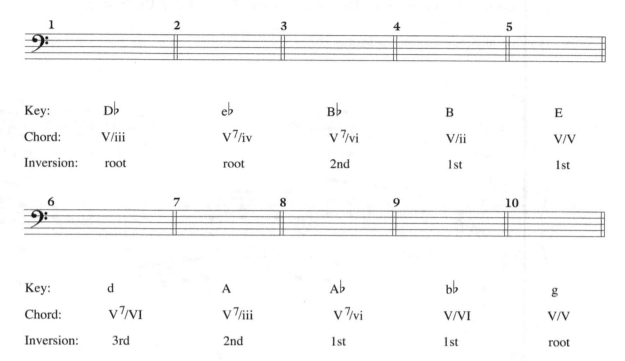

	1	2	3	4	5
Key:	D♭	e♭	B♭	B	E
Chord:	V/iii	V⁷/iv	V⁷/vi	V/ii	V/V
Inversion:	root	root	2nd	1st	1st

	6	7	8	9	10
Key:	d	A	A♭	b♭	g
Chord:	V⁷/VI	V⁷/iii	V⁷/vi	V/VI	V/V
Inversion:	3rd	2nd	1st	1st	root

1F. Provide Roman numeral analysis.

1   Rodgers and Hammerstein: "Do-Re-Mi" (from *The Sound of Music*)

(Circled pitches are nonchord tones)

2   Schumann: Carnaval op. 9 (no. 4: "Valse noble")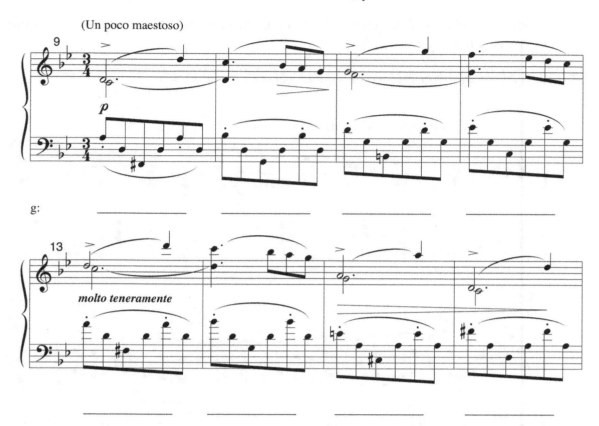

g:

3   Beethoven: Piano Sonata op. 13 (second movement)

A♭:

1G. Provide harmonic analysis, and answer the additional questions.

1   Circle and label all NCTs. Describe the rhythmic effect produced in mm. 20–21. What musical
      elements reinforce it?

Tchaikovsky: Piano Concerto no. 1, op. 23 (first movement) 🔊

Andante non troppo e molto maestoso

Key ___: _____ _____ _____

rit.

___ ___ ___ ___ X ___ ___ ___ ___

2   J. S. Bach: Prelude no. 8 from _Well-Tempered Clavier_ I 🔊

eᵇ:

3   Draw arrows showing the resolution of each tonicizing tritone.

Beethoven: Symphony no. 1, op. 21 (first movement) 🔊

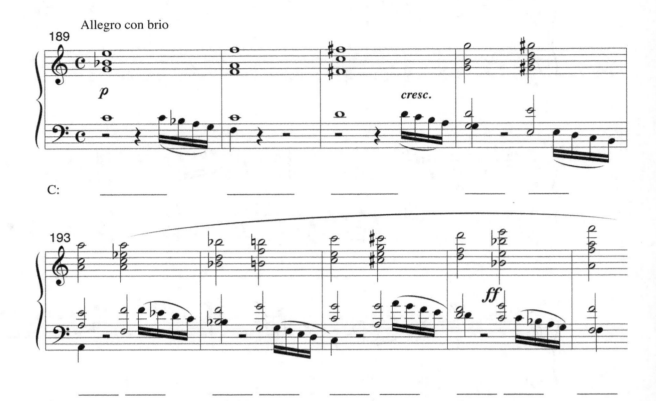

2. SECONDARY LEADING TONE CHORDS

2A. Give the Roman numeral that expresses the chord's function in each key.

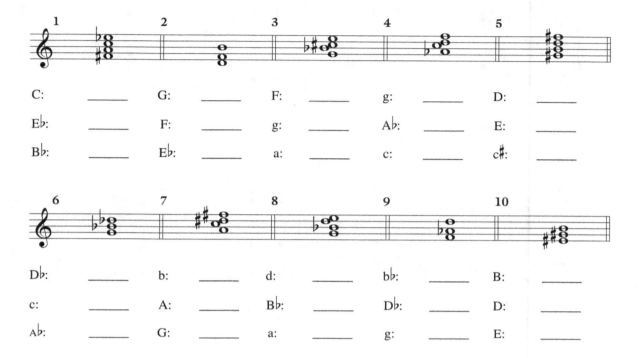

C: _____	G: _____	F: _____	g: _____	D: _____
Eb: _____	F: _____	g: _____	Ab: _____	E: _____
Bb: _____	Eb: _____	a: _____	c: _____	c#: _____

Db: _____	b: _____	d: _____	bb: _____	B: _____
c: _____	A: _____	Bb: _____	Db: _____	D: _____
Ab: _____	G: _____	a: _____	g: _____	E: _____

2B. Add the key signature and construct the specified chords.

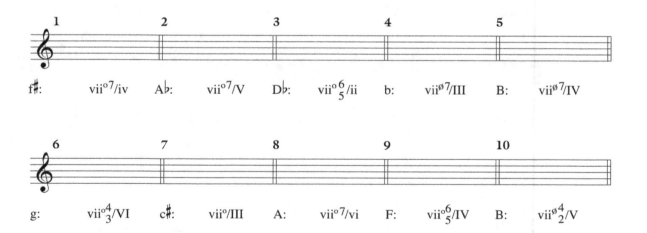

f#: vii°7/iv   Ab: vii°7/V   Db: vii°6/5/ii   b: viiø7/III   B: viiø7/IV

g: vii°4/3/VI   c#: vii°/III   A: vii°7/vi   F: vii°6/5/IV   B: viiø4/2/V

2C. Provide harmonic analyses. Assume the first chord to be the tonic.

Key ___: __ __ __   __: __ __ __   __: __ __ __   __: __ __ __   __: __ __ __

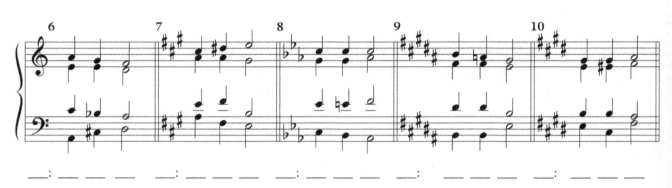

__: __ __ __   __: __ __ __   __: __ __ __   __: __ __ __   __: __ __ __

2D. Choose the chord that would best harmonize the middle pitch in each melodic pattern. Place its symbol beneath the chord, and write the chord on the lower staff. Consider the first chord to be the tonic. Two possible answers exist for Nos. 1, 5 and 7. Choose either answer.

viio7/vi   **V/V**   **viio7/iii**   **viio6/ii**

viiø7/V   **V7/IV**   **V/vi**   **viio7/iv**

D: ___   Bb: ___   F: ___   Ab: ___   f#:   ___

B: ___   G: ___   C: ___   g: ___   Gb: ___

2E. Provide harmonic analysis.

1   Haydn: String Quartet op. 76, no. 3 (second movement)

2   Beethoven: Piano Sonata op. 14, no. 2 (second movement)

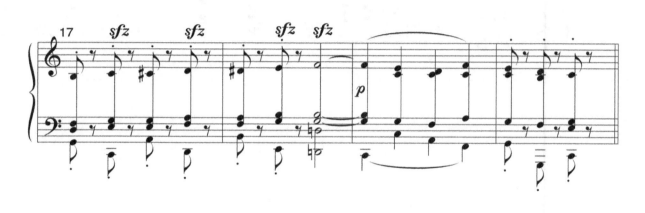

2F. Provide harmonic analysis of the excerpts that follow, and answer the additional questions.

1   Describe and symbolize the melodic form of the excerpt. Identify all examples of varied
     repetition, and explain what is varied. How does Mozart use dynamics in this regard? What
     makes the final phrase longer than the others? Examples of simultaneous NCTs occur. Identify
     them.

Mozart: Piano Sonata K. 311 (second movement)

Key ___: _____

2   Chopin: Impromptu, op. 29

Key _____ : _____ _____ _____ _____

3. VOICE LEADING

3A. Resolve the following chords. Then provide harmonic analysis.

Eb: ___ ___   D: ___ ___   G: ___ ___   Bb: ___ ___   Db: ___ ___

c: ___ ___   b: ___ ___   e: ___ ___   g: ___ ___   bb: ___ ___

A: ___ ___   Ab: ___ ___   Bb: ___ ___   E: ___ ___   C: ___ ___

f#: ___ ___   f: ___ ___   g: ___ ___   c#: ___ ___   a: ___ ___

3B. Add the key signature. Then, part write and resolve the secondary functions in four voices. Provide the analysis symbols for the resolution chord.

Eb: V_3^4/IV ___   d: vii°⁷/iv ___   A: V_2^4/ii ___   Db: V/iii ___   f#: vii°$_5^6$/VI ___

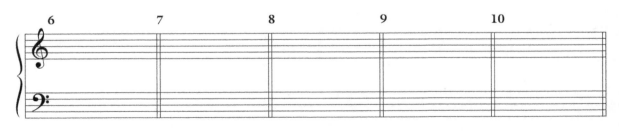

Ab: viiø$_3^4$/V ___   E: V_5^6/V ___   B: V_3^4/vi ___   g: vii°$_2^4$/iv ___   Gb: V⁶/iii ___

3C. Complete the following in four voices as indicated. In certain cases, it may be necessary to use less common doublings in order to resolve the altered tones properly.

3D. Realize the following figured bass line and provide a harmonic analysis.

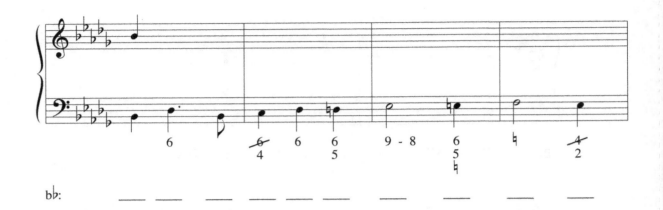

bb: ___ ___ ___ ___ ___ ___ ___ ___

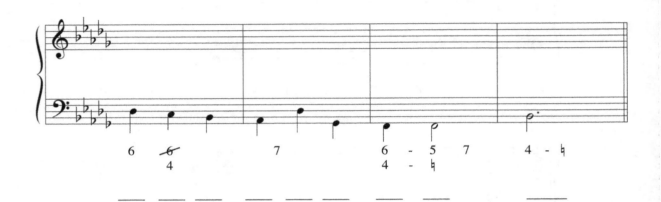

___ ___ ___ ___ ___ ___ ___ ___

CHAPTER SIXTEEN
Secondary Function II

1. JAZZ AND POPULAR STYLES

1A. Notate the chords indicated by the lead-sheet symbols. Then, symbolize the tonicizing chord group in the given key, in the manner shown in Example 16-4 of your text.

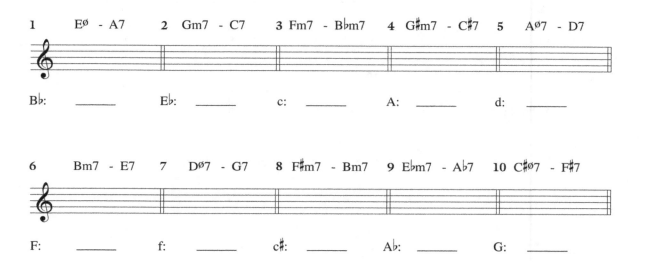

1 Eø - A7   2 Gm7 - C7   3 Fm7 - B♭m7   4 G♯m7 - C♯7   5 Aø7 - D7

B♭: _____   E♭: _____   c: _____   A: _____   d: _____

6 Bm7 - E7   7 Dø7 - G7   8 F♯m7 - Bm7   9 E♭m7 - A♭7   10 C♯ø7 - F♯7

F: _____   f: _____   c♯: _____   A♭: _____   G: _____

1B. In the first measure, complete a two-chord tonicization by preceding the given chord with a ii7
(iiø7) *or* following it with a V7, whichever is required. In the second measure, follow this
tonicizing chord group with the appropriate chord. Provide harmonic analysis. Place the Roman
numeral of the tonicized chord beneath the first line, with the tonicizing chord group above.

i.e.

1C. Show the tonicizing chord groups in the following excerpts, using the method for symbolizing those groups presented in this chapter. NOTE: Some symbols in Example 1 (in mm. 2, 6, and 13) reflect chord alterations not yet discussed. For now, disregard these additions to the basic symbol.

1 **Johnny Mercer and David Raksin: "Laura" (theme from the motion picture *Laura*)** 🔊

Show 5 tonicizing chord groups

2   **Lionel Bart: "Where is Love?"** (from *Oliver*, act 1, no. 7)

Show 6 tonicizing chord groups

1D. Add lead-sheet chord symbols above the following melody. Then write the bass line suggested by the analysis symbols.

Quincy Jones: "Quintessence"

Medium Ballad

1E. Add the key signature, and notate the pair of tonicizing chords.

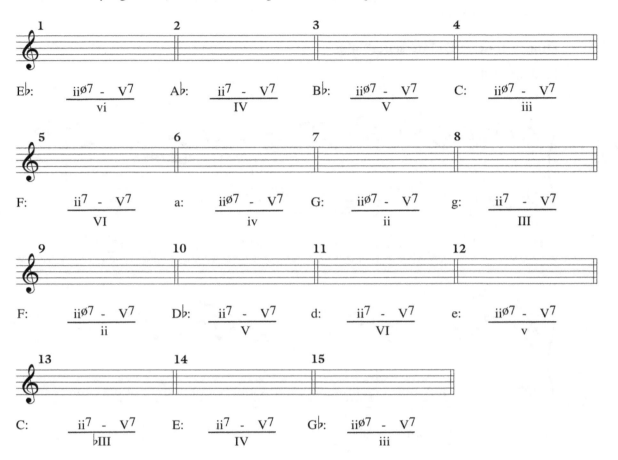

Eb: iiø7 - V7   Ab: ii7 - V7   Bb: iiø7 - V7   C: iiø7 - V7
           vi   IV   V   iii

F: ii7 - V7   a: iiø7 - V7   G: iiø7 - V7   g: ii7 - V7
           VI   iv   ii   III

F: iiø7 - V7   Db: ii7 - V7   d: ii7 - V7   e: iiø7 - V7
           ii   V   VI   v

C: ii7 - V7   E: ii7 - V7   Gb: iiø7 - V7
          bIII   IV   iii

1F. The melodies that follow contain strategically placed harmonies. Create tonicizing chord
     groups leading to or incorporating these harmonies. (Consider the melodic sequences present.)
     Notate the chords on the lower staff, and add to the lead-sheet symbols above the melody.
     (As with simple tonicizations, the tonicized chord need not always follow.)

2

3

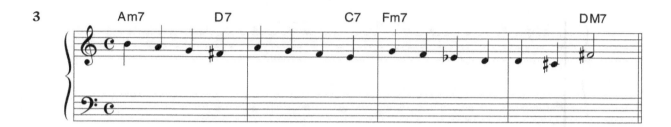

2. MELODY HARMONIZATION

2A. Analyze the harmonic implications in the following two-voice passages. The given notes constitute the root, third, or fifth of a triad, or perhaps the seventh of a seventh chord. Determine the most appropriate harmonies. Be alert to possible secondary functions. After adding Roman numerals, part write the inner voices.

c:

2B. Provide harmonizations for the melodies. Incorporate secondary functions where possible. Use inversion to create a more melodic bass. Place lead-sheet symbols above the melody, and notate the figured bass line on the staff beneath it.

2C. Provide Roman-numeral analysis of the passages that follow, and answer the specific questions that precede each.

1   **Reginald Lucas and James Matume: "The Closer I Get to You"**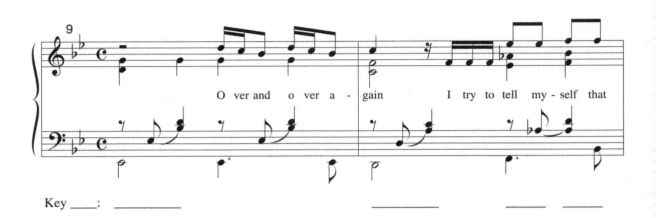

Add lead-sheet chord symbols and show tonicizing chord groups.

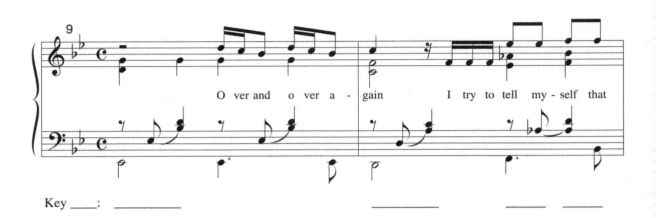

Key ____: _____   _____   _____

2 Bill Evans: "Turn Out the Stars" 🔊

Symbolize tonicizing chord groups, placing the chord group above the line and the letter name of the tonicized scale degree beneath the line, as described in the chapter.

CHAPTER SEVENTEEN
Modulation I

1. MODULATION BY COMMON CHORD

1A. List four keys in which each of the following chords is diatonic, and indicate the chord's function in each of those keys.

Example:	c#	*B: ii*	*c#: i*	*g#: iv*	*A: iii*
1	F#	_____	_____	_____	_____
2	c	_____	_____	_____	_____
3	B	_____	_____	_____	_____
4	g	_____	_____	_____	_____
5	eb	_____	_____	_____	_____
6	Bb	_____	_____	_____	_____
7	d	_____	_____	_____	_____
8	a	_____	_____	_____	_____
9	E	_____	_____	_____	_____
10	Ab	_____	_____	_____	_____

1B. List the keys closely related to each given key. Indicate which key would be suggested by the consistent appearance of the accidentals shown to the right. (Assume these accidentals to be the *only* ones that appear.)

Example	Key	Closely Related Keys	Accidentals	Key Implied
	F	d, B♭, g, C, a	B, C♯	d
1	D♭	_____	G, E	_____
2	e	_____	D, f, G♯	_____
3	B♭	_____	F♯	_____
4	c♯	_____	B	_____
5	d	_____	C, E♭	_____
6	E	_____	D	_____
7	B	_____	E♯	_____
8	G♭	_____	C, D	_____
9	b	_____	E♯, G♯, A	_____
10	A♭	_____	G♭	_____

1C. On separate manuscript paper, realize the following bass lines and provide Roman numeral analysis, including the dual function of the common chord.

1D. In the melodies that follow, indicate *where* the modulation occurs, identify the most likely position of the pivot chord, and place a Roman numeral beneath the melody at that point showing a possible dual harmonic function for the pivot chord.

3

Bright

mf

1E. Complete the four-part passages. Modulate by pivot chord to the specified key, using a pivot that functions as a pre-dominant in the new key. Provide complete harmonic analysis.

1

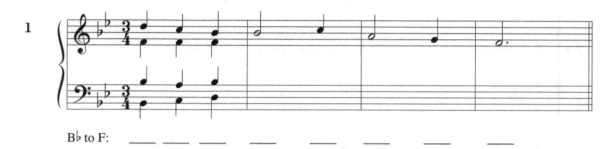

B♭ to F: ___ ___ ___ ___ ___ ___ ___

2

f to A♭: ___ ___ ___ ___ ___

3

D to b: ___ ___ ___ ___ ___ ___

4

A♭ to c: ___ ___ ___

2. CHROMATIC MODULATION

2A. Assuming the music to begin in the key of the first chord and end in the key of the last chord, label each modulation as pivot chord or chromatic. If a pivot chord modulation, also indicate the dual harmonic function of the pivot.

1   **P.C. or Chromatic?** _____   **P.C. function Old:** ____   **New:** ____

2   **P.C. or Chromatic?** _____   **P.C. function Old:** ____   **New:** ____

3   **P.C. or Chromatic?** _____   **P.C. function Old:** ____   **New:** ____

4   **P.C. or Chromatic?** _____   **P.C. function Old:** ____   **New:** ____

5   **P.C. or Chromatic?** _____   **P.C. function Old:** ____   **New:** ____

2B. Provide Roman-numeral analysis. Identify the modulations as either common chord or chromatic. If common chord, indicate its dual harmonic function. Be sure to indicate the old and new keys.

1

Key ___: __ __ __ __ __ __ __ __ __ __ __

2

Key ___: __ __ __ __ __ __ __ __ __ __ __

3

Key ___: __ __ __ __ __ __ __ __ __

4

Key ___: __ __ __ __ __ __ __ __

2C. Realize the figured bass lines for four voices. Provide harmonic analysis, identifying the modulation in each.

1

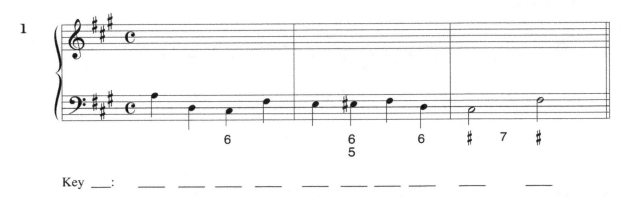

Key ___: __ __ __ __ __ __ __

2

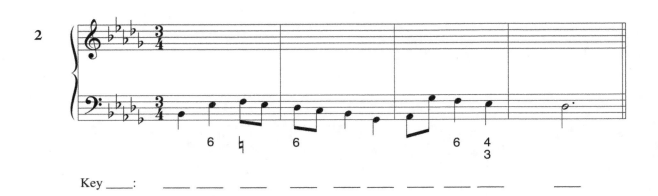

Key ___: __ __ __ __ __ __ __

3

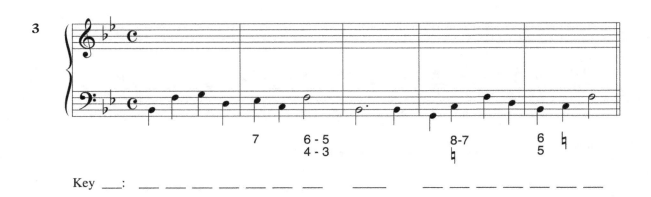

Key ___: __ __ __ __ __ __ __ __

2D. Complete the following passages, employing chromatic modulations to the specified keys. The complete passage should comprise four measures, and the modulation should occur soon enough to establish the new key. Provide complete harmonic analysis.

1

Modulate to F

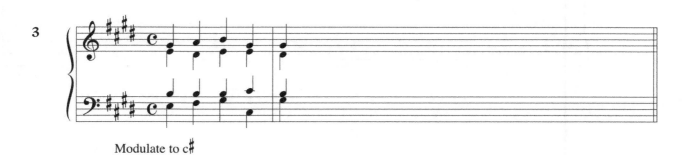

2

Modulate to e

3

Modulate to c♯

4

Modulate to c

2E. Harmonize the melody, including at least one modulation.

    1.   Place the Roman numeral for each harmony in the blank provided. (The blanks suggest an appropriate number of harmonies, but you may add others.)

    2.   On the bass staff, lightly notate the bass line created by the harmonies. Then, create a more melodic bass through inversion and passing tones. (Avoid second inversion except for standard six-four chords.)

    3.   Identify the modulation as either pivot chord or chromatic.

D:

2F. Provide a complete harmonic analysis and supply the requested additional information concerning the excerpt that follows.

1. The modulation occurs in m. ___.

2. An escape tone can be found in m. __ and m. __.

3. An anticipation can be found in m. __.

4. A 4–3 suspension with ornamented resolution appears in m. __.

5. Describe the phrase structure. Identify the type of period if one is present.

6. Look up the term "Sarabande," and identify the elements of that dance evident in the music.

Bach: *French Suite* **no. 6, BWV 817 (Sarabande)**

2G. Provide complete harmonic analysis. Indicate whether the modulation is a common-chord or chromatic type. For the former, identify the common chord and show its dual harmonic function.

1   J. S. Bach: "O Gott, du frommer Gott" 🔊

E: _____ _____ _____ _____ _____ _____ _____ _____ _____

2   Beethoven: Piano Sonata op. 90 (first movement) 🔊

Key: _____ _____ _____ _____ _____ _____ _____ _____

_____ _____ _____ _____ _____ _____ _____

3   Mozart: Piano Sonata K. 332 (first movement) 🔊

Key: _____   _____   _____

_____   _____   _____

_____   _____   _____

2H. 1.   Provide harmonic analysis.

      2.   Identify all sequences and describe them.

      3.   Identify the modulations as common-chord or chromatic.

      4.   Identify the phrases, and label them to show their relationships.

J.S. Bach: "Ich steh'mit einem Fuss im Grabe" (from Cantata 156)

CHAPTER EIGHTEEN

The Art of Countermelody

1. THE BASICS OF TWO-VOICE COUNTERPOINT

1A. For the Handel Allegro:

1. Between the staves, indicate the interval formed on each downbeat. How many of each occur: imperfect consonances ___? perfect consonances ___? dissonances ___?

2. Circle all dissonances (seconds, fourths, and sevenths) in the right-hand part, and label them (PT, NT, and so on).

3. Which type of embellishing dissonance appears most often in the passage? _____

Handel: *Suites de Pieces pour le Clavecin*, second collection (no. 3: Allegro) 🔊

1B. For the Bach Gavotte that follows:

1. Between the staves, indicate the interval formed on each downbeat. How many of each occur: imperfect consonances ___? perfect consonances ___? dissonances ___?

2. Circle all dissonances (seconds, fourths, and sevenths). Dissonances appear in both the upper and lower voice. Normally, the voice with the longer note is the chord tone.

3. Identify an example of each: 1:1 counterpoint; 2:1 counterpoint; 4:1 counterpoint.

4. Bracket and label any harmonies clearly arpeggiated in the right-hand part.

J.S. Bach: Gavotte I from English Suite no. 3, BWV 808

1C. For the excerpt that follows:

    1. Place a P (Parallel), S (Similar), O (Oblique), or C (Contrary) in each blank to indicate the type of motion created by the two voices. Which type of motion predominates?
       _____

    2. Which species of counterpoint–1:1 or 2:1–predominates?

    3. Between the staves, indicate with a number (1–8) the interval formed on each downbeat. How many of each occur: imperfect consonances ___? perfect consonances ___? dissonances ___?

    4. Circle and label all dissonances (PT, NT, and so on).

    5. Bracket and label with an L each occurrence of a leap in both voices.

    6. Describe the distribution of rhythmic activity between the two voices: a) evenly distributed ___ b) Soprano more active ___ c) Bass more active ___

Handel: Sonata for Flute and Continuo, op. 1, no. 5, HWV 363b (Bourée) 🔊

1D. In the blanks, provide harmonic analysis of the figured bass line. Then create a 1:1 counterpoint
     against the bass line, using your harmonic analysis as a guide. Use only consonances and sevenths,
     as suggested by the figured bass and your analysis.

Handel: Sonata no. 3 for Flute and Continuo (Alla Breve)

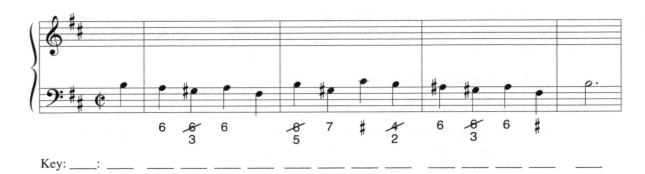

Key: ____: ____ ____ ____ ____ ____ ____ ____ ____ ____ ____ ____ ____

1E. On the blank staves, convert the given counterpoint as directed.

   1   Convert to 2:1 counterpoint by adding standard embellishing tones or additional
       consonances to one voice or the other.

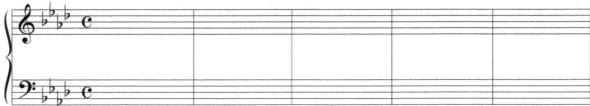

2   Convert to 4:1 counterpoint by adding standard embellishing tones and/or additional consonances to the upper voice. Create a cadence in m. 4 on beat 3, and then resume eighth-note activity.

1F. Compose a counterpoint against the given melody so that the species is consistently 2:1. In other words, plot eighth notes against quarter notes and quarter notes against eighth notes.

1G. Retaining the bass line, write three variations above it by creating first a 2:1 counterpoint, then 3:1, and finally 4:1. For the first variation, simply embellish the given melody. For the next two, you either may retain the melody tones or not, as you wish.

Pachelbel: Canon in D

2.   J. S. BACH'S CHORALE HARMONIZATIONS

2A.   Nonchord tones have been removed from the following chorale harmonizations. Enliven the counterpoint by inserting standard NCTs in any appropriate voice. It's best to avoid embellishing more than one voice simultaneously.

1   J. S. Bach: "O Haupt voll Blut und Wunden" 🔊

HINT: Bach's version contains a 9–8 SUS, PTs, NTs, and a double ANT ornamented by a LN (m. 6).

2   **J. S. Bach: "Wachet auf, ruft uns die Stimme"**

HINT: Bach's version contains extra chord tones, PTs (single and double) in the soprano and elsewhere, NTs (including an UN in m. 4), and a chain suspension (in the alto).

2B.   Provide harmonic analysis. Then, embellish the counterpoint by adding nonchord tones. (Bach's have been removed.)

1   **J. S. Bach: "Jesu, deine tiefen Wunden"**

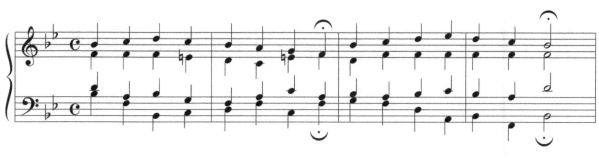

Key ___: ___ ___ ___ ___ ___ ___ ___ ___ ___ ___ ___ ___ ___

2 J. S. Bach: "Befiehl du deine Wege"

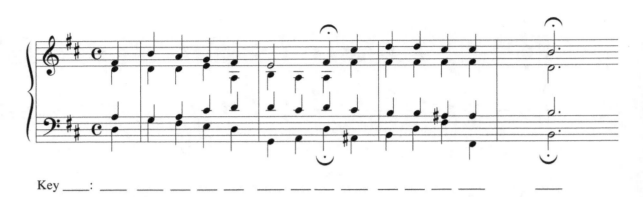

Key ___: ___ ___ ___ ___ ___ ___ ___ ___ ___ ___ ___ ___

3. J.S. BACH'S TWO-PART INVENTIONS

3A. Identify the contrapuntal techniques applied to the motive. (In some cases, more than one technique has been applied simultaneously.)

Motive:

a _____ b _____ c _____

d _____ e _____

3B. Perform the requested operations on the given motive.

Motive:

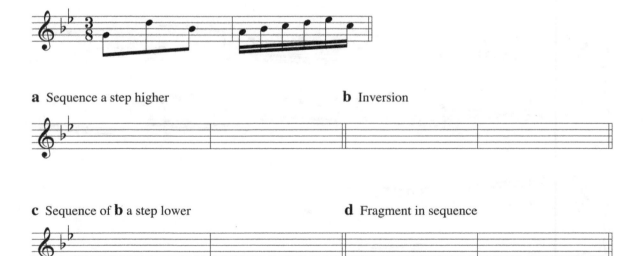

a Sequence a step higher   **b** Inversion

c Sequence of **b** a step lower   **d** Fragment in sequence

3C. Answer the following questions concerning the excerpt.

1. What single term describes the relationship between mm. 7–8 and 9–10? _____
    Locate another four-bar segment with the same relationship._____

2. Locate an example of inverted counterpoint. _____

3. Which of the contrapuntal devices listed on page 312 are represented at the following points:

    a. m. 8 (left hand): _____
    b. m. 11 (right hand): _____
    c. m. 15 (right hand): _____

4. Provide Roman numeral analysis of the implied harmonies. Analyze one chord per measure
    except for m. 17.

J. S. Bach: Two-Part Invention no. 4, BWV 775

3D. Indicate the harmonies most likely implied in the following excerpts. Then, circle and identify all embellishing tones.

1 J. S. Bach: Suite no. 1 for Violoncello, BWV 1007 (Corrente)

G: _____ _____ _____ _____

_____ _____ _____ _____

2 Anonymous (Notebook for Anna Magdelena Bach): Menuet

g: _____ _____ _____ _____

_____ Bb: _____ _____ _____

3   J. S. Bach: Suite no. 1 for Violoncello, BWV 1007 (menuet II)

4   Anonymous (Notebook for Anna Magdelena Bach): Menuet

3E. In the following passage, locate by measure number and voice (*u*pper or *l*ower) the points at which the indicated techniques may be found.

NOTE: Only simple intervals are used in designating pitch levels of sequences and imitation. (For example, imitation at the twelfth below would be designated as imitation at the fifth below.)

1. Imitation a fourth below _____

2. Imitation a fourth above _____

3. Imitation a fifth below _____

4. Imitation an octave below _____

5. Chain suspension (the resolution of one suspension becomes the preparation for the next) _____

6. Modified sequence a fifth below _____

7. Tonal sequence a second below _____

Handel: "Halle" Sonata no. 1 for Flute and Continuo, HWV 8

3F. Identify all contrapuntal techniques employed. For sequences and imitation, indicate the pitch level of the repetition. Indicate whether sequences are real or tonal.

J. S. Bach: Fugue no. 10 from *The Well-Tempered Clavier I*

3G. Analyze the invention that follows.

1. Identify the motive and, if present, the countermotive.

2. Identify points where the counterpoint has been inverted.

3. Identify prominent examples of melodic inversion, imitation, and sequence.

4. Diagram the tonal plan.

5. Locate one example of extended imitation between the two parts.

J. S. Bach: Two-Part Invention no. 14, BWV 785

CHAPTER NINETEEN
The Fugue

A.   Identify the answers to the subjects as real or tonal. If an answer is tonal, identify the note or notes that make it so.

1   Handel: Fugue op. 6, no. 3, HWV 607

Subject

Answer

2   J. S. Bach: Fugue no. 5 from *The Well-Tempered Clavier II*

Subject

Answer

3   A. Scarlatti: Sonata a Quattro

Subject

Answer

4   Mozart: Fantasy and Fugue in C, K. 394

Subject

Answer

5   J. S. Bach: Fugue no. 7 from *The Well-Tempered Clavier I*

Subject

Answer

B. 1.   Provide an answer to the given subject.

    2.   In mm. 5–8: Against the answer, compose a countersubject of mostly 2:1 counterpoint
          that implies functional harmonies.

    3.   Follow with an inverted counterpoint of the answer and its countersubject.

1. Answer here:

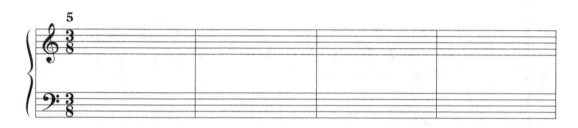

2. Countersubject against answer

3. Inverted counterpoint of preceding four measures, transposed to a minor:

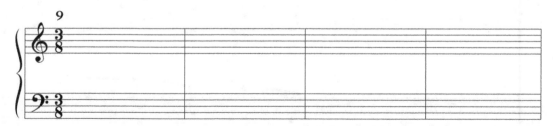

C.   For the following fugue expositions:

1.   Bracket and label with S or A all subject and answer statements.

2.   Indicate whether the answers are real or tonal.

3.   Indicate whether the music accompanying the answer appears to constitute a counter-subject.

4.   Describe any motivic relationships between the subject its counterpoint.

1   Johann Pachelbel: Fugue in C Major 🔊

2   J.S. Bach: Fugue no. 17 from *The Well-Tempered Clavier I* 🔊

D. An excerpt from a four-voice fugue by J. S. Bach follows. Determine the length of the subject and mark all appearances of the subject (S) and answer (A). Then answer these questions.

1. The exposition ends in m. ___. A clear cadence follows the exposition at m. ___. What type of cadence is this? _____ The order of entries is _____.

2. The answer is _____ (real or tonal?).

3. A countersubject _____ (is or is not) present.

4. After the exposition, the next group entry occurs between m. ___ and m. ___.

5. *Stretto* occurs at m. ___ and m. ___.

6. The first episode of the fugue begins at m. ___ and ends at m. ___ with a _____ (what cadence?).

7. The primary developmental technique employed in this episode is _____.

8. The excerpt ends in the key of ____.

9. A third group entry appears in mm. ___—___. This group contains entries at: _____.

10. Compare mm. 16–17 and mm. 19–20, and describe Bach's use of invertible counterpoint in these measures.

J. S. Bach: *The Well-Tempered Clavier, II,* BWV 878 (Fugue no. 9)

E.   Provide analytic markings for the fugue that follows.

1.   In the exposition, identify all entries of the subject and answer. Identify a countersubject, if one is present. Mark the end of the exposition.

2.   Identify all subsequent appearances of the subject.

3.   Identify the more prominent cadences, and indicate the key in each case.

4.   Diagram the tonal plan, naming and locating the most important tonalities established.

5.   Describe the contrapuntal techniques employed in the episodes.

J. S. Bach: *The Well-Tempered Clavier, I,* **BWV 847 (Fugue no. 2)**

F. Provide analytical markings for the fugue that follows, using the analysis of Bach's Fugue no. 16 (page 330 and following) as your guideline.

1. In the exposition, identify all entries of the subject and answer, along with the countersubject if one is present. Clearly identify the end of the exposition.

2. Identify all subsequent appearances of the subject. (Some of the entries are slightly modified.) Note any occurrences of stretto.

3. Identify three prominent cadences aside from the final cadence. Indicate both the key and cadence type.

4. Diagram the tonal plan, naming and locating the most important tonalities established.

5. Describe the contrapuntal techniques employed in mm. 30–36.

J. S. Bach: Fugue no. 11 from *The Well-Tempered Clavier I*

CHAPTER TWENTY
Mixing Modes

1. CHANGE OF MODE AND MODAL BORROWING

1A. Using textbook Example 20-4 as a reference, name the key or keys in which each of the following chords would function as a borrowed harmony. Indicate borrowed functions by Roman numeral. Observe the clef.

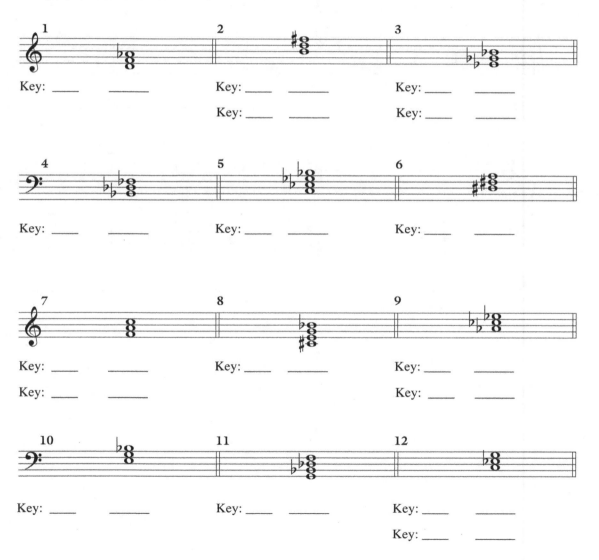

Key: ____ ____

Key: ____ ____
Key: ____ ____

Key: ____ ____
Key: ____ ____

Key: ____ ____

Key: ____ ____

Key: ____ ____

Key: ____ ____
Key: ____ ____

Key: ____ ____
Key: ____ ____

Key: ____ ____

Key: ____ ____

Key: ____ ____
Key: ____ ____

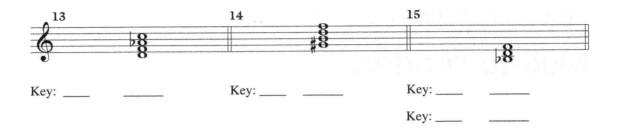

Key: ____   ____   Key: ____   ____   Key: ____   ____

                                                  Key: ____   ____

1B. Identify the key in which each chord functions as one of the common borrowed harmonies,
     and indicate its function by Roman numeral. Then resolve the chord.

Key ___: ____ ____ __: ____ ____ __: ____ ____ __: ____ ____

Key ___: ____ ____ __: ____ ____ __: ____ ____ __: ____ ____

1C. Illustrate the borrowed harmonies. Place the chords, unvoiced, in root position on the single staff provided.

1 B♭: Borrowed submediant

2 A♭: Borrowed supertonic

3 D: Borrowed subdominant

4 F: Borrowed leading tone seventh

5 G: Borrowed supertonic seventh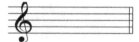

6 D♭: Borrowed subdominant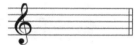

7 E: Borrowed submediant

8 E♭: Borrowed supertonic

9 C: Borrowed leading tone seventh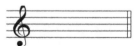

10 A: Borrowed subdominant

1D. Realize in four voices the following figured bass lines.

Then, provide harmonic analysis.

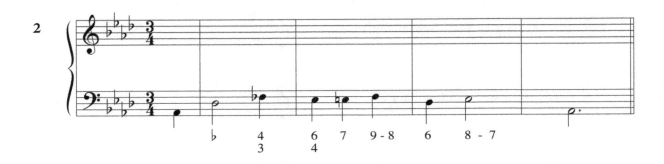

1E. Part-write the following soprano lines, altering the given chords on repetition (mm. 3–4) to create as many borrowed harmonies as you can. Voice-leading will determine which and how many borrowed harmonies are possible in each passage. Provide harmonic analysis.

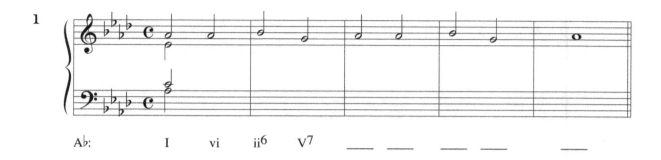

Ab: I   vi   ii⁶   V⁷   __ __   __ __   __

E: I   IV⁶   V   I   __   __   __   __

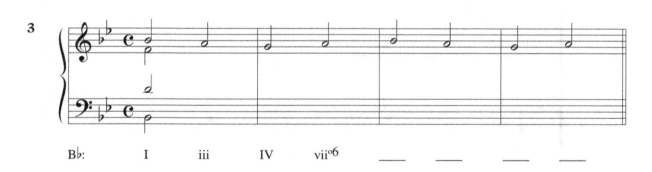

Bb: I   iii   IV   vii°⁶   __   __   __   __

A: I V vi ii⁶ V I⁶ IV I   __ __ __ __   __ __ __ __

1F. Harmonize the following melodic passages in four voices, using mode mixture in the manner specified. Then provide harmonic analysis.

1   Use a borrowed leading-tone seventh chord and a borrowed pre-dominant.

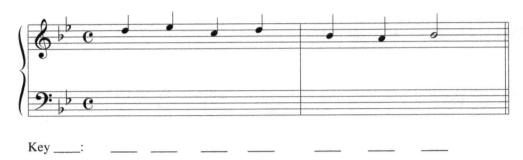

Key ___: __ __ __ __   __ __ __

2   Use the borrowed submediant.

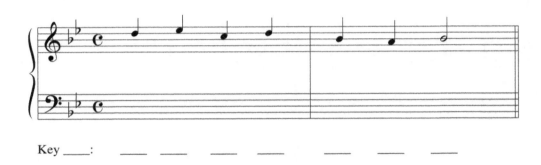

Key ___: __ __ __ __   __ __ __

3   Use two appropriate borrowed harmonies.

Key ___: __ __ __   __ __ __   __ __   __

1G. Provide harmonic analysis of the following excerpts. Describe the root relationships in mm. 79–83. Disregard for now the chords marked with an X.

1   Haydn: Piano Sonata H. XVI:27 (first movement)

2   Schubert: Impromptu op. 142, no. 2 🔊

3   Fred Rogers: "Won't You Be My Neighbor" 🔊

2.   CHROMATIC-THIRD RELATIONSHIPS

2A.   Regarding the first triad of each pair as the tonic, add beneath the second chord the Roman numeral that properly expresses the type of third relationship (bIII, VI, and so on).

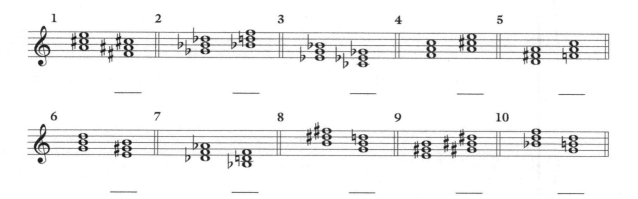

2B.   Part-write in four voices the specified chromatic-third relationship to each chord. Retain the common tone in the same voice and blacken it in both chords. Be sure to observe the inversions indicated.

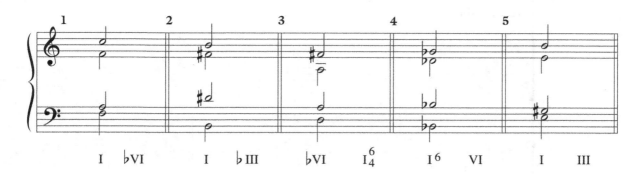

2C. Write the following chromatic-third relationships for four voices.

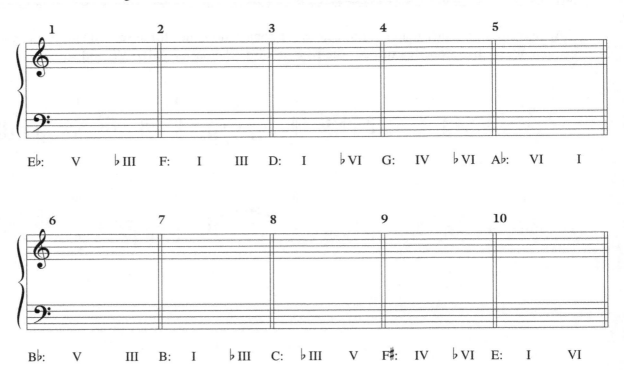

2D. Realize the figured bass. Then, provide harmonic analysis, using symbols that reflect the type of chromatic-third relationship.

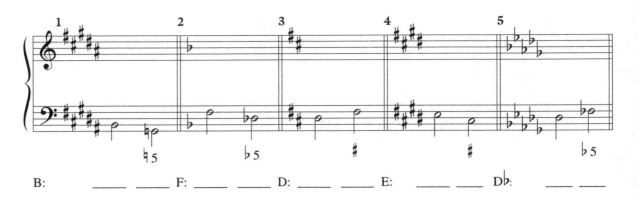

2E. Realize the following figured bass lines for four voices. Try to retain the common tone in the same voice between chromatically third-related chords. Then provide harmonic analysis.

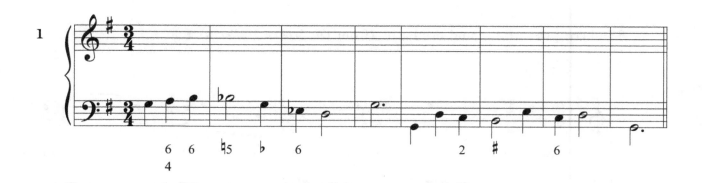

1

6 6 ♮5 ♭ 6   2 ♯ 6
        4

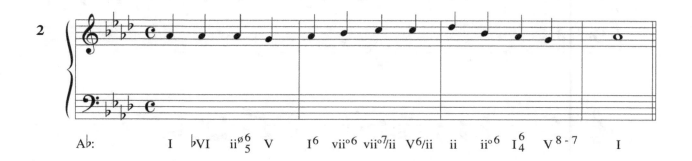

2

A♭:   I ♭VI ii^{ø6}₅ V   I⁶ vii°⁶ vii°⁷/ii V⁶/ii ii ii°⁶ I⁶₄ V^{8 - 7}   I

2F.   Provide harmonic analysis of the following excerpt. Show all key changes, and identify chromatic-
      third relationships that occur between keys and between chords.

Schubert: "Der Müller und der Bach" (from *Die Schöne Müllerin*) 🔊

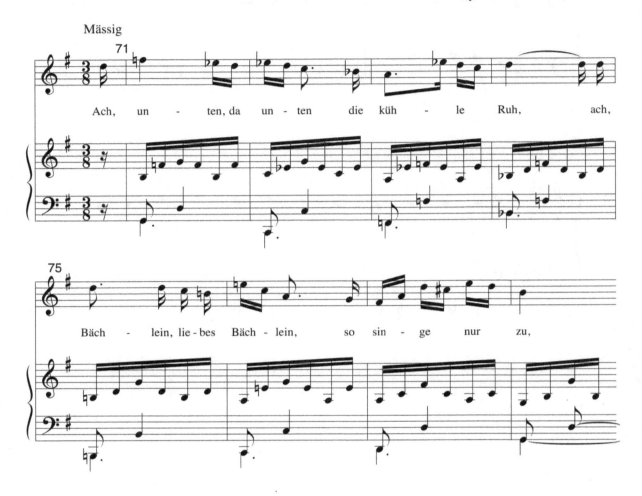

2G. Provide the requested information concerning the excerpts that follow.

1   Brahms: Piano Sonata op. 1 (fourth movement) 🔊

1. Identify the four tonalities suggested.

2. Identify all diatonic- and chromatic-third relationships between tonalities.

3. Locate and describe an example of mode mixture.

Note: The chord in mm. 179–181 is discussed in Chapter 21. Disregard it for now.

2 Wagner: "Elsas Traum" from *Lohengrin* (Act One, Scene II) 🔊
(Piano transcription: Franz Liszt)

Provide complete harmonic analysis, and answer the following questions:

1. The excerpt begins in A♭ and quickly modulates, coming to a cadence in m. 42. In what key does the music cadence? _____ Through what intermediate tonality is this key related to A♭? _____ Explain precisely the tonal relationship between the beginning and ending of this first phrase.

    _____

2. What term describes the harmonic technique found on beat 4 of m. 41? _____

3. Locate the next occurrence of this technique. m. _____

4. By what chromatic chord does Wagner return to A♭? _____

2H. Provide harmonic analysis of the passage that follows. Your analysis should identify—in this order—a chromatic-third relationship, a tonicizing chord group, and a secondary dominant (not yet resolved).

Leslie Bricusse and Anthony Newley: "Goldfinger" Arr. R.T.

I.   Answer the following questions regarding the music that follows:

1.   Identify two chords that are in chromatic-third relationship.

2.   Identify a change of mode.

3.   Locate a modulation and the common chord if one is present.

4.   Diagram the melodic phrase/period structure, identifying the phrase relationships in the manner described in Chapter 9.

5.   Compare the music in the first eight measures with that in the last eight measures.

6.   Using Roman numerals, symbolize the relationship between the opening key and the key to which the passage modulates.

7.   Provide complete harmonic analysis.

Rossini: "Domine Deus" (no. 4 from _Petite Messe Solennelle_)

CHAPTER TWENTY-ONE
Altered Pre-Dominants

1. THE NEAPOLITAN SIXTH CHORD

1A. Write the N6 in the indicated *minor* keys, filling in (blackening) the altered tone in each case.

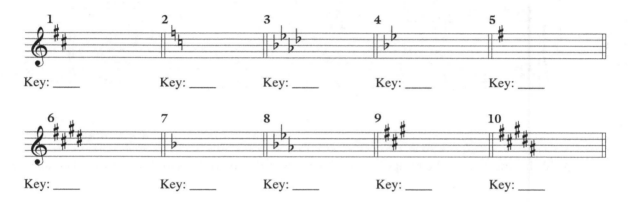

Key: ____   Key: ____   Key: ____   Key: ____   Key: ____

Key: ____   Key: ____   Key: ____   Key: ____   Key: ____

1B. Indicate the minor key in which each chord would be the Neapolitan sixth chord. If *not* a Neapolitan sixth chord, place an X in the blank.

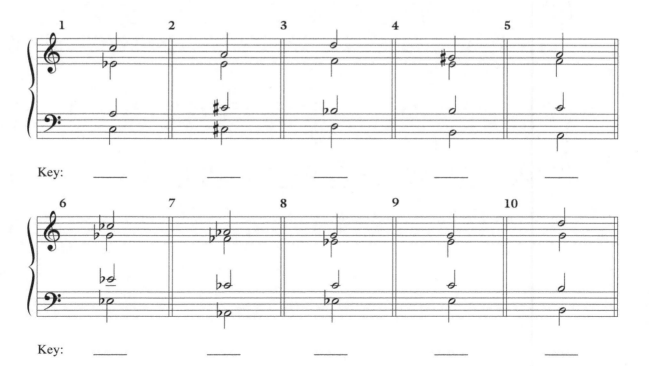

Key: _____   _____   _____   _____   _____

Key: _____   _____   _____   _____   _____

1C. Determine the minor key, and add the key signature. Then, precede the given dominant with a Neapolitan sixth chord, observing correct part-writing principles.

1D. Write and resolve the Neapolitan sixth chords in the minor keys indicated by the key signatures.

1E. Add the key signature, and provide three resolutions for the given Neapolitan sixth chords.

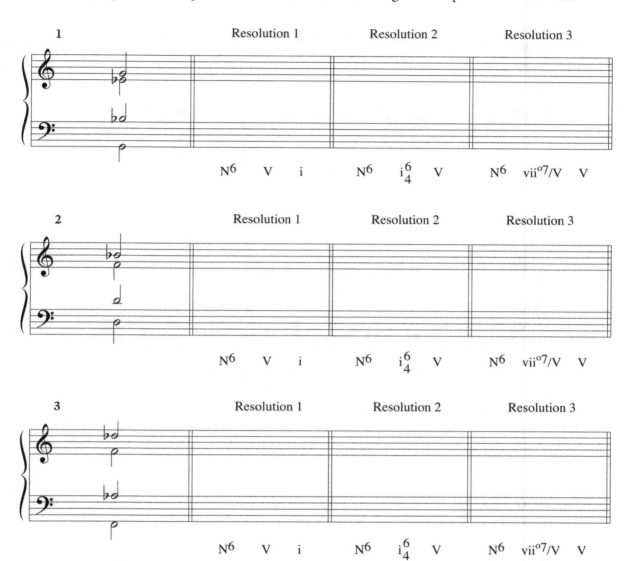

260 ALTERED PRE-DOMINANTS

1F. Add soprano, alto, and tenor voices to the figured bass lines. Then provide harmonic analysis.

a:

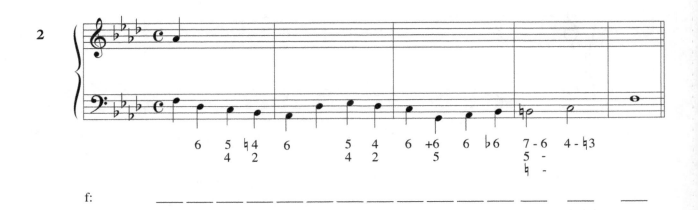

f:

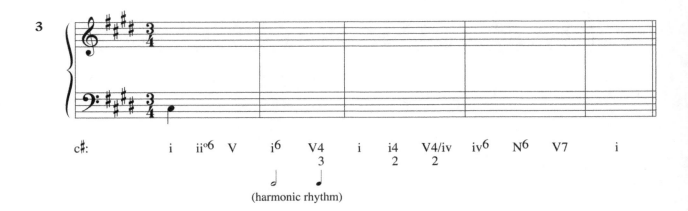

c#: i ii°6 V i6 V4/3 i i4/2 V4/2/iv iv6 N6 V7 i

(harmonic rhythm)

1G. Provide harmonic analysis of the excerpts that follow.

1   Mozart: Piano Sonata K. 280 (second movement)

2   Schubert: "Der Müller und der Bach" (from *Die Schöne Müllerin*)

Note: This excerpt begins in B♭ and modulates. Decide where to change keys.

3   Brahms: Sonata for Clarinet and Piano, op. 120, no. 1 (first movement) 🔊

4   Haydn: Piano Sonata H. XVI: 37 (first movement) 🔊

1H. Identify all harmonies, sequences, large-scale arpeggiations, and step progressions in the following passage.

Bizet: "Votre toast, je peux vous le rendre" (from *Carmen*) 🔊

2. AUGMENTED SIXTH CHORDS

2A. Identify each chord as an Italian, French, German sixth, or enharmonic German sixth chord.

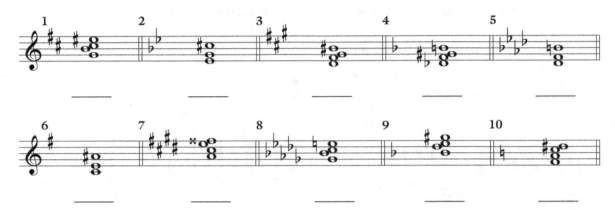

2B. In the blanks, add the key and the chord symbol for the given harmony. Then, resolve the chord.

2C. Identify the type of altered pre-dominant chord (N6, It+6, Fr+6, or Gr+6) and the key in which it appears. Add the key signature and resolve the chord.

Key ___: _____ ____ ____ ___: ____ ____ ____ ___: ____ ____ ____ ___: ____ ____ ____ ___: ____ ____ ____

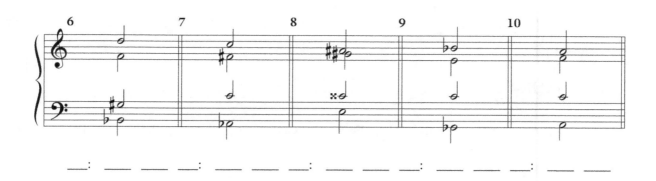

___: ____ ____ ____ ___: ____ ____ ____ ___: ____ ____ ____ ___: ____ ____ ____ ___: ____ ____ ____

2D. Place the chord symbol in the upper blank. (Assume minor keys.) Then add the single accidental that would turn the chord into an augmented sixth chord. In the second blank, identify the type (It+6, Fr+6, or Gr+6).

Chord Symbol: _____   _____   _____   _____

Type of +6th: _____   _____   _____   _____

Chord Symbol: _____   _____   _____   _____

Type of +6th: _____   _____   _____   _____

2E. Add the key signatures and construct the indicated chords. Fill in note heads to show the tendency tone(s), and write the note(s) of resolution.

Example:

d: N⁶   It+⁶   Fr+⁶   Gr+⁶

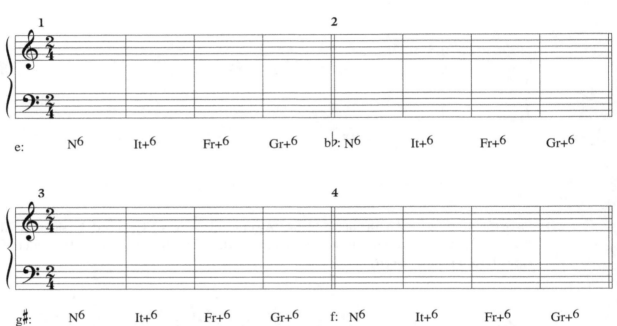

1   2

e: N⁶   It+⁶   Fr+⁶   Gr+⁶   b♭: N⁶   It+⁶   Fr+⁶   Gr+⁶

3   4

g♯:   N⁶   It+⁶   Fr+⁶   Gr+⁶   f: N⁶   It+⁶   Fr+⁶   Gr+⁶

2F.   Part write the figured bass lines and provide harmonic analysis.

1

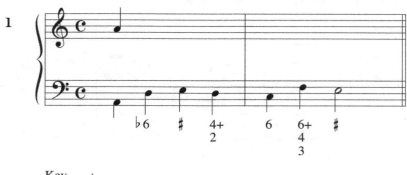

Key ___: ___ ___ ___ ___   ___ ___ ___

2

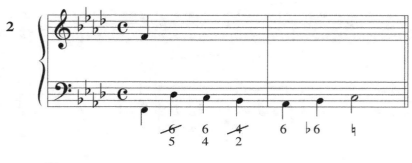

Key ___: ___ ___ ___ ___   ___ ___ ___

3

Key ___: ___ ___ ___ ___   ___ ___ ___

4

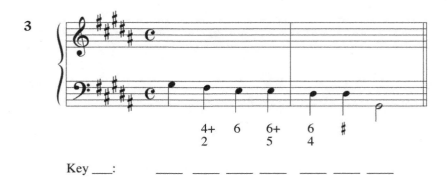

Key ___: ___ ___ ___ ___   ___ ___ ___

2G. Provide harmonic analysis.

1   Beethoven: Symphony no, 5, op. 67 (first movement) 🔊

(Allegro con brio)

2   Grieg: Piano Concerto op. 16 (first movement) 🔊

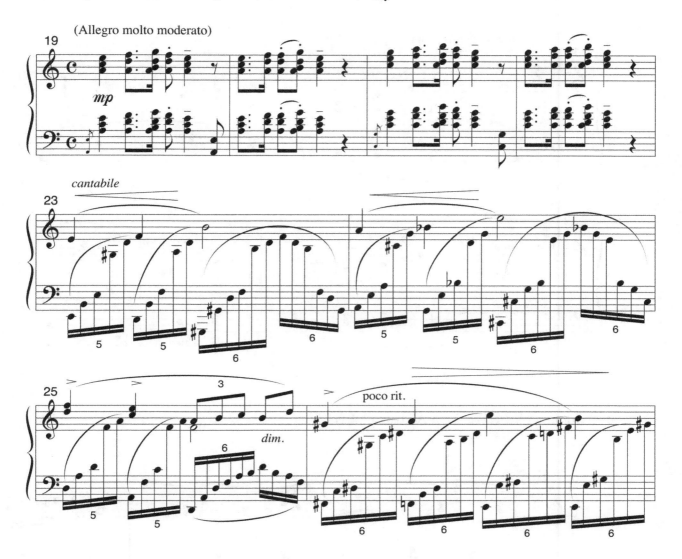

3   Beethoven: Piano Sonata op. 109 (third movement) 🔊

4   Joplin: "A Breeze from Alabama" 🔊

CHAPTER TWENTY-TWO

Other Chromatic Harmonies

1. ALTERED DOMINANTS

1A. Give the key and chord symbol for each altered dominant.

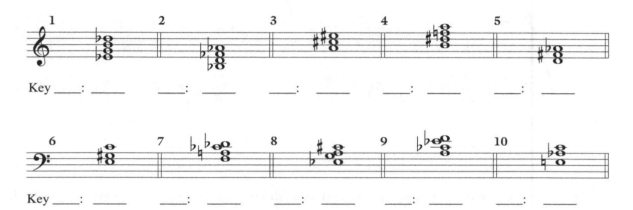

Key ____: ____   ____: ____   ____: ____   ____: ____   ____: ____

Key ____: ____   ____: ____   ____: ____   ____: ____   ____: ____

1B. Add the notes indicated by the figured-bass symbols. Then provide the most likely analysis symbol for each altered dominant. Consider that the key signatures might indicate a major or a minor key, and the chord itself might be a *secondary* altered dominant.

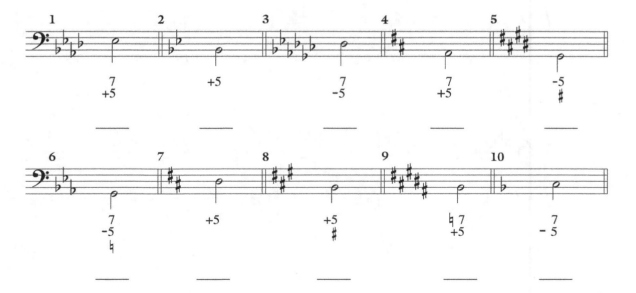

1C. Provide the Roman numeral symbol that identifies each chord's function. Then resolve the chord.

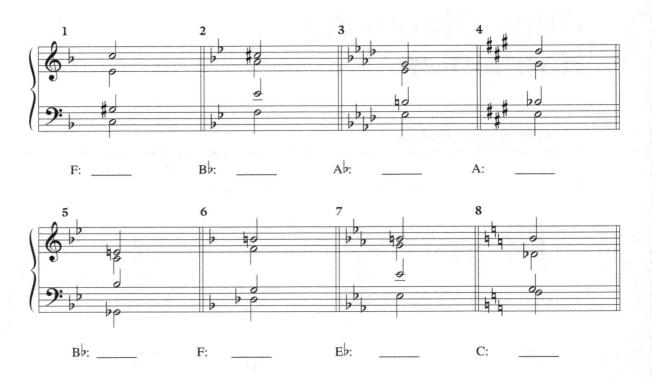

F: _____   Bb: _____   Ab: _____   A: _____

Bb: _____   F: _____   Eb: _____   C: _____

1D. Alter each dominant or secondary dominant to produce the indicated chord and resolve it.

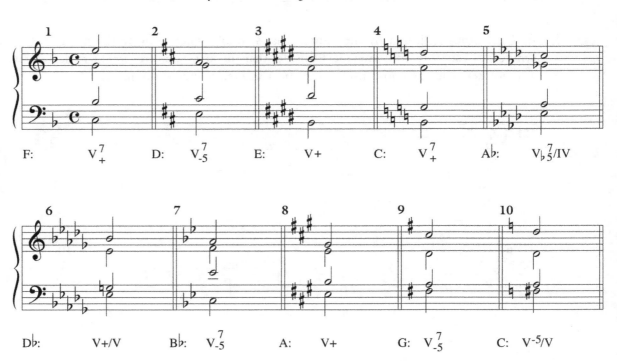

F: V⁷₊   D: V⁷₋₅   E: V+   C: V⁷₊   Ab: V♭⁷₅/IV

Db: V+/V   Bb: V⁷₋₅   A: V+   G: V⁷₋₅   C: V⁻⁵/V

1E. Add the signature for the key in which each chord would function as indicated. Then construct the chord in four-voice structure and resolve.

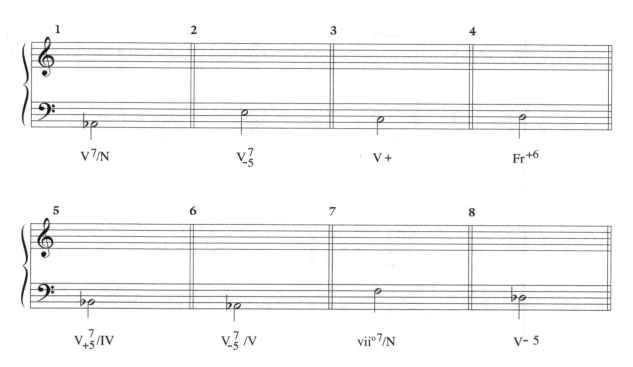

1F. Provide harmonic analysis. Disregard circled tones.

1   Brahms: Symphony no. 4, op. 98 (fourth movement)

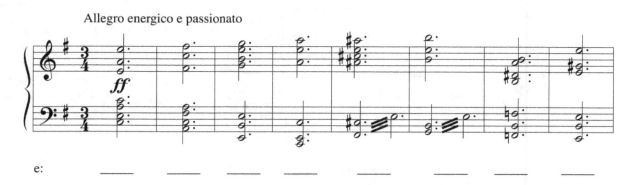

2   Schumann: Albumblätter, op. 99

A:

c#:

3   Jerome Kern: "Smoke Gets in Your Eyes"

1G. Answer these questions concerning the excerpt that follows.

1. Describe and symbolize the phrase structure of mm. 53–68.

2. Locate an example of hemiola in the melodic line.

3. Identify the harmonic technique that takes place at m. 69.

4. Locate and name the borrowed harmony that appears between m. 53 and m. 68.

5. A Neapolitan sixth chord appears in m. ___. A secondary leading-tone seventh chord appears in m. ___ and is symbolized ___. A secondary dominant seventh chord appears in m. ___ and is symbolized ___. An altered dominant appears in m. ___ and is symbolized ___.

Chopin: *Grand Valse Brillante,* op. 34, no. 2 🔊

2. EMBELLISHING DIMINISHED SEVENTH CHORDS

2A. Identify and resolve the embellishing diminished seventh chords. The resolution chord is either
I or V (either $\hat{1}$ or $\hat{5}$ will be a common tone).

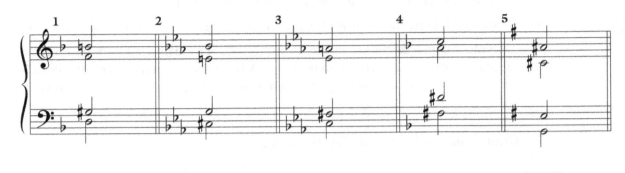

2B. In four voices, write the embellishing diminished seventh chord in the inversion and voicing
that would most properly precede the given chord. Then add analysis symbols.

2C. Part write the following for four voices.

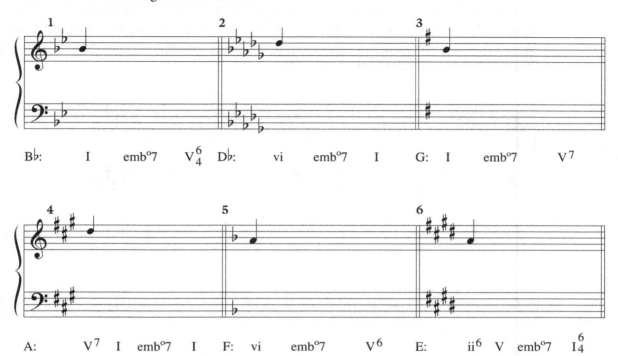

Bb: I emb°7 V$^6_4$ Db: vi emb°7 I G: I emb°7 V^7

A: V^7 I emb°7 I F: vi emb°7 V^6 E: ii^6 V emb°7 I$^6_4$

2D. Harmonize the following melodic passages using an embellishing diminished seventh chord at the point indicated.

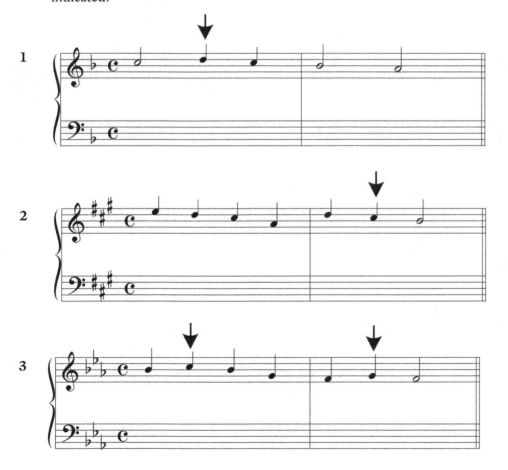

2E. Precede the given tonic, dominant, or dominant seventh first with its embellishing diminished seventh chord and then with a functional diminished seventh chord, inverted and voiced to produce the best voice leading. Remember that, with the embellishing diminished seventh chord, the smoothest voice leading will often produce nonstandard doubling in the embellished chord. Add Roman numerals.

B♭: ___ ___ ___ ___   D: ___ ___ ___ ___   E: ___ ___ ___ ___

F: ___ ___ ___ ___   E♭ ___ ___ ___ ___   C: ___ ___ ___ ___

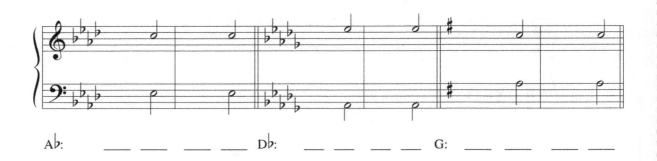

A♭: ___ ___ ___ ___   D♭: ___ ___ ___ ___   G: ___ ___ ___ ___

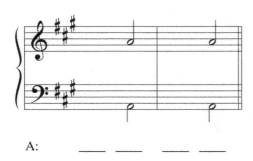

A: ___ ___ ___ ___

2F. Provide harmonic analysis. You should be able to identify an embellishing diminished seventh chord, an altered dominant, and a tonicization in each example.

1   Schubert: Piano Sonata op. 53 (second movement) 🔊

2   Tchaikovsky: Piano Concerto no. 1 (first movement) 🔊

CHAPTER TWENTY-THREE

Modulation II

1. RECOGNIZING SIGNALS

1A. For the tonality in the first column, name the tonality suggested by the consistent appearance of the pitches in the second column.

Original Key	Pitches	Implied Tonality
1. F	E♭, A♭	_____
2. e	F♮, G♯, D♮	_____
3. D♭	B♮, G♮, D♮	_____
4. g	A♭, E♭, B♮, F♮	_____
5. A	F♮, C♮, G♮	_____
6. ♭	A♮	_____
7. f♯	G♮, C♮, E♮	_____
8. B♭	D♭, A♭, G♭	_____
9. E♭	E♮, D♭	_____
10. B	A♮, B♯	_____

1B. The following melodies begin in one key and modulate to another. They *do not* necessarily come to a cadence on the new tonic. Identify the beginning tonality and the new tonality, and explain specifically what features of the melody suggest the new key.

1

Beginning tonality: _____   Ending tonality: _____

Features suggesting new key: _____

2

Beginning tonality: _____   Ending tonality: _____

Features suggesting new key: _____

3

Beginning tonality: _____   Ending tonality: _____

Features suggesting new key: _____

1C. The following two-part passages imply a modulation. Provide a harmonic analysis and add the two inner voices.

1

Key ____: _   _

2

Key ____: _   _

2.   BACK TO THE TONAL BORDER

2A. Realize the following figured bass lines. Then provide a harmonic analysis and describe the type of modulation present.

1

Type of Modulation: _____

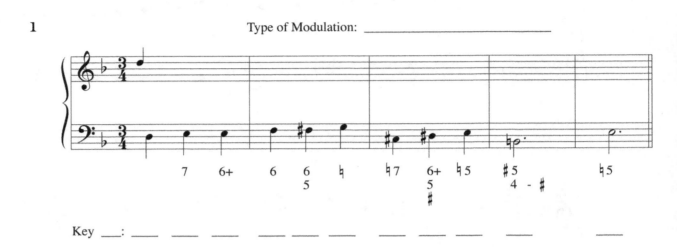

Key ___: ___ ___ ___ ___ ___ ___ ___ ___ ___ ___

2

Type of Modulation: _____

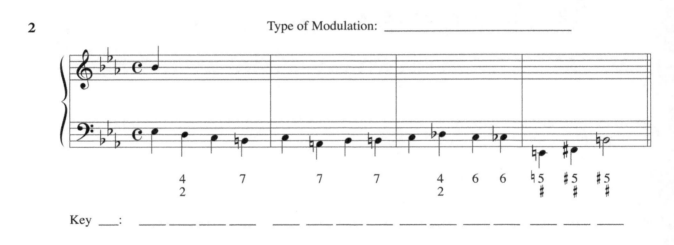

Key ___: ___ ___ ___ ___ ___ ___ ___ ___ ___ ___ ___

3

Type of Modulation: _____

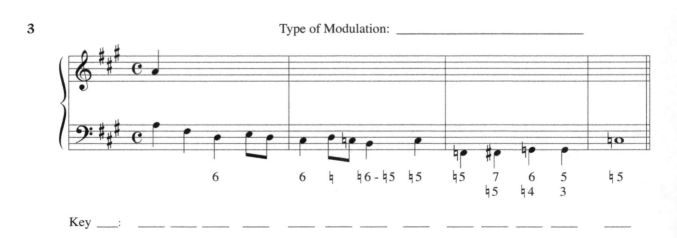

Key ___: ___ ___ ___ ___ ___ ___ ___ ___ ___ ___

2B.   1.   Name the beginning tonality.

2.   Two tonality changes occur. Locate them, and list the accidentals that suggest the changes.

3.   Locate cadences, and identify them.

4.   Identify all "clue chords."

Haydn: Piano Trio, H. XV:18 (first movement) 🔊

2C. Answer these questions concerning Haydn's String Quartet op. 74, no. 3.

1. In what key does the passage begin? _____

2. At m. 26, a modulation occurs. What is the new key? _____ What type of modulation is this? _____

3. What chord symbol is most appropriate for m. 28, beats 3–4? _____ Discuss the voice leading from this chord.

4. In mm. 34–35, the music modulates again. To what key? ____ Provide harmonic analysis for these two measures.

5. What chord symbol is most appropriate for the chord in m. 36? _____

6. In what key is the music at m. 38? ____ What is the relationship of this key to the immediately preceding key? _____

Haydn: String Quartet op. 74, no. 3 (second movement) 🔊

3. THE SECRET LIVES OF CHORDS

3A. Respell the following dominant seventh chords as German sixth chords and resolve them.
Include all accidentals, as key signatures are not given.

3B. Respell the following German sixth chords as dominant seventh chords and resolve them.
Include all accidentals, as key signatures are not given.

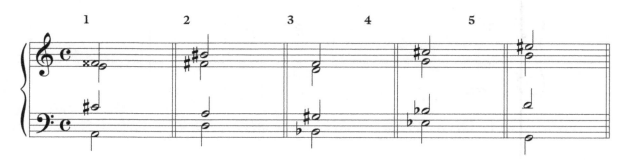

3C. In each diminished seventh chord, lower by one half step the chord member necessary to transform the chord into a dominant seventh chord in the key shown. Then resolve the chord and provide the analysis symbols.

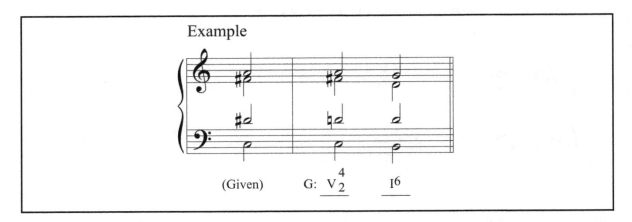

(Given)   G: V$_2^4$ I^6

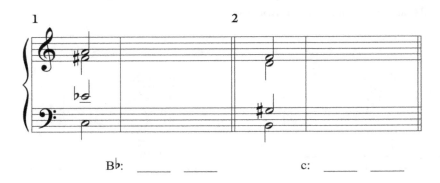

1   2

B♭: _____ _____   c: _____ _____

3   4

G♭: _____ _____   e: _____ _____

3D. *Without changing the voicing of the given chord,* lower the bass note by one half step and respell enharmonically any other pitches necessary to create a German sixth chord. Then, resolve it, adding accidentals, as needed.

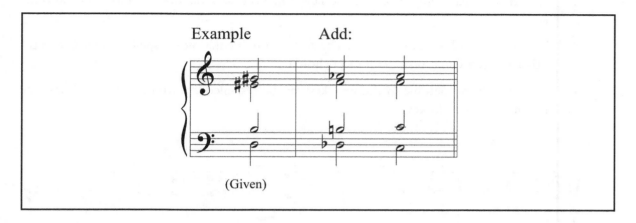

Example   Add:

(Given)

1   2

3   4

3E. For the following modulations, choose the single best description.

1. A common chord is present.

2. A borrowed harmony in one of the keys functions as a diatonic harmony in the other key.

3. The pivot chord is diatonic in one key and, through enharmonic spelling, diatonic in the other key (an enharmonic common chord).

4. The first chord diatonic in the new key can be respelled enharmonically as a borrowed harmony in the old key.

3F. Provide harmonic analysis and answer the specific questions.

1   Beethoven: Sonata for Horn and Piano, op. 17 (first movement) 🔊

The chord in m. 34 appears two more times in the excerpt. (Think enharmonically.) Identify its function at each appearance.

2   **Brahms: "An eine Äolsharfe", op. 19, no. 5** 🔊

This excerpt modulates away from the starting key and back to it.

1.   In the first modulation, which chord has a "secret life" as explained in Part Three of the chapter? _____ What is the dual harmonic function of this chord? Old key: ___ New Key: ___ Is this modulation, a chromatic ___ or common chord ___ type?

2.   Diminished seventh chords appear in four measures. Give the best Roman numeral designation for each, and characterize each as functional or embellishing.

          m. ___   R.N.: ___   Functional ___ Embellishing ___

          m. ___   R.N.: ___   Functional ___ Embellishing ___

          m. ___   R.N.: ___   Functional ___ Embellishing ___

          m. ___   R.N.: ___   Functional ___ Embellishing ___

3.   A chromatic modulation accomplishes the return to the beginning tonality. Locate and describe the chromatic pivot. (Think enharmonically.): m.___ Old key: ___ New key: ___

4.   What kind of cadence ends the passage? _____ Give Roman numerals that reflect the two chords creating the cadence. _____ _____

5.   What is the relationship of the two keys in the passage? (Think enharmonically.)
       _____

3G. Provide a complete analysis of the following song. In your analysis:

1.   Identify melodic motives.

2.   Identify one or more of each of the following types of harmonic chromaticism:

    1.   A Neapolitan sixth chord _____

    2.   A French sixth chord_____

    3.   A change of mode _____

    4.   Secondary function _____

    5.   A modulation involving mode mixture _____

    6.   Chromatic-third relationship between chords _____

    7.   Chromatic-third relationship between tonalities_____

    8.   A modulation in which a chord functions as an enharmonically spelled borrowed harmony in the old key and as a diatonic chord in the new key_____

    9.   Chromatic modulations_____

GENERAL HINT: Some of these harmonic techniques occur several times. Nevertheless, you should be able to find them *in the order listed* by working from the beginning of the song toward the end.

Schubert: "Die Liebe hat Gelogen," D.751

CHAPTER TWENTY-FOUR

Harmonic Extensions and Chromatic Techniques

1. TRIADIC EXTENSIONS

1A. Construct a dominant-major ninth or dominant-minor ninth chord, as appropriate to the key indicated.

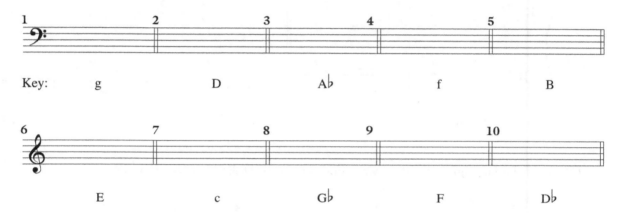

1B. Identify the key in which each chord functions as a dominant ninth or thirteenth chord. Add the key signature, resolve the chord, and add appropriate analysis symbols.

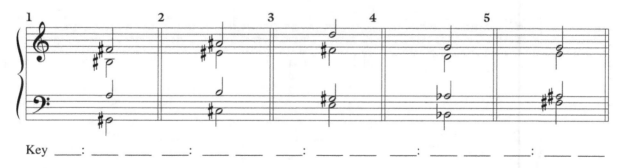

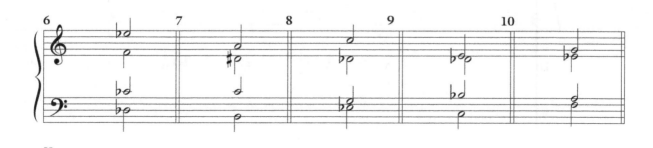

1C. Write in four voices the requested ninth or thirteenth chord, voiced so that the ninth and thirteenth resolve into the given chord.

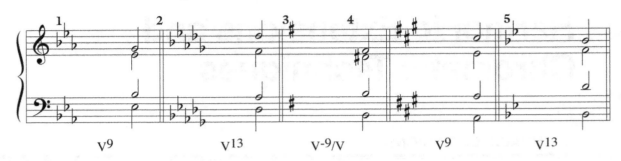

V⁹   V¹³   V⁻⁹/V   V⁹   V¹³

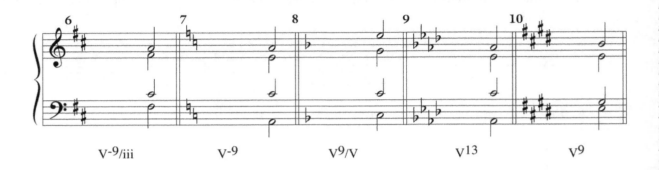

V⁻⁹/iii   V⁻⁹   V⁹/V   V¹³   V⁹

1D. Add the key signature, then write and resolve the following harmonies.

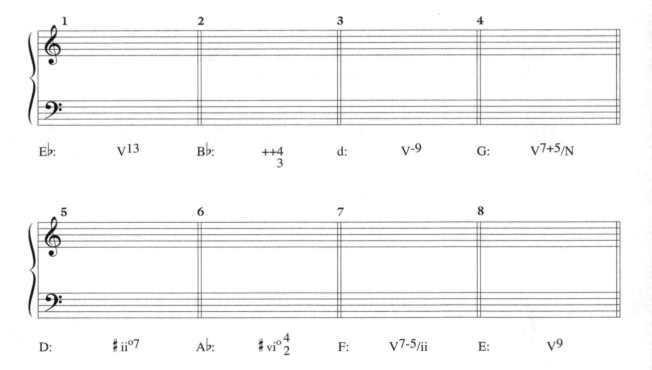

E♭:   V¹³   B♭:   ++$^{+4}_{3}$ d: V⁻⁹   G: V⁷⁺⁵/N

D: ♯ii°⁷   A♭:   ♯vi°$^{4}_{2}$ F: V⁷⁻⁵/ii   E: V⁹

1E. Provide harmonic analysis of the passages that follow.

1   Chopin: Valse op. 64, no. 2

Key: _____: _____

2   Fauré: "Apres un Reve", op. 7, no. 1

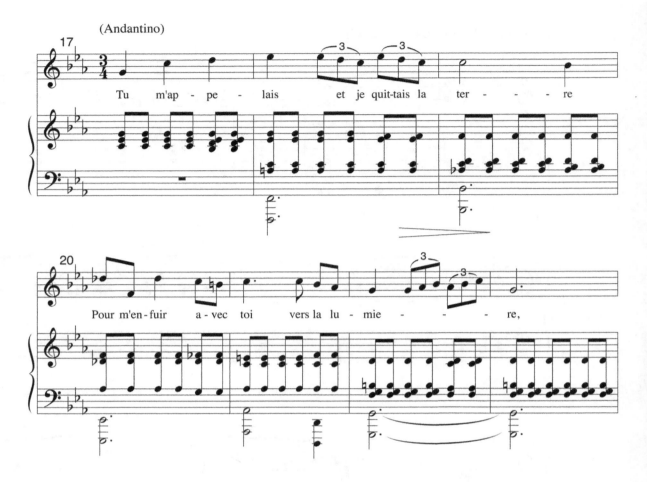

1F.   Add lead-sheet symbols in the blanks. (Determine the chords from the point indicated by the blanks.) Then, list the measures in which the following chord types appear.

1.   Dominant-minor ninth with thirteenth: _____

2.   Minor seventh chord: _____

3.   Major seventh chord: _____

4.   Major ninth chord: _____

5.   Minor eleventh chord: _____

6.   Dominant thirteenth chord: _____

Bill Evans: "Very Early" 🔊

Medium Waltz

2   LINEAR CHROMATICISM

2A. The following figured bass line can be realized so that each of the upper lines moves chromatically. Realize the passage in this manner and provide harmonic analysis.

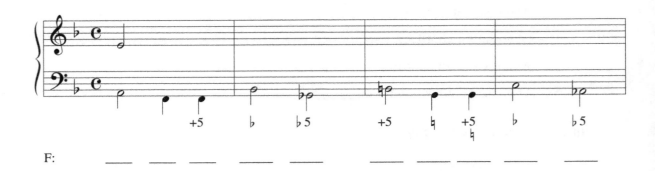

F:

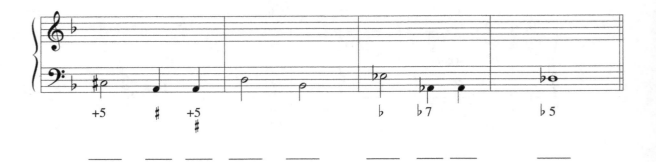

2B. 1. Add soprano, alto and tenor voices to the figured bass in such a way that each voice ascends chromatically from its first pitch to its last. Some of the resulting linear harmonies will be functional and others will not.

2. Place a V+, V7, or V above each chord that has that structure. Then, bracket all V-I motions. Place "Gr+6" beneath the one chord that functions enharmonically in this way.

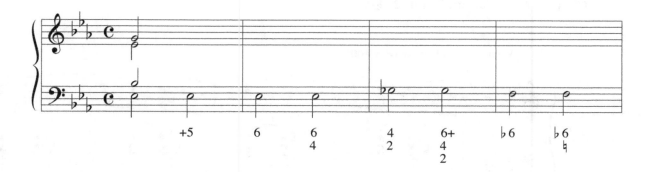

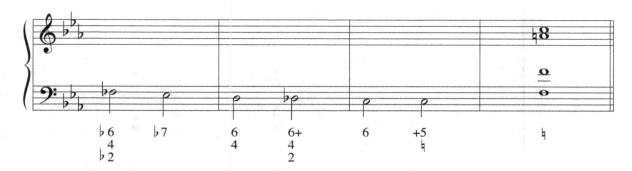

2C. Provide harmonic analysis of the passage that follows. In your analysis:

1.   Identify tonicizing chord groups.

2.   Identify linear chromaticism.

3.   Identify with the proper symbol chromatic harmonies previously studied.

Chopin: Mazurka op. 7, no. 2

3. HARMONIC SEQUENCE

3A. Create an exact harmonic sequence by repeating the given idea at the indicated transposition level. Then, provide a meaningful harmonic analysis, showing tonicizing chord groups where appropriate.

3B.   Provide harmonic analysis. Show tonicizations using the method described in the chapter. Identify all harmonic sequences. (The left-hand part in mm. 21–24 shows how far removed Chopin's music is from the Baroque four-part style.)

Chopin: Mazurka op. posth. 67, no. 2 🔊

3C. Identify and describe the harmonic sequences, and answer the additional questions.

1   Mozart: Minuet, K. 355 🔊

Discuss the melodic form of the passage.

2   Chopin: Ballade no. 2, op. 38

Add harmonic analysis in the blanks provided. Which chord members are omitted in the thirteenth chord? Which members of the chord resolve, and to what do they resolve?

3   Liszt: "Vallee d'Obermann" (from Années de Pèlerinage (Book I)) 🔊

1.   What are the two keys in the "piu lento?" ___ and ___ .

2.   Identify the first chord ____ and the chord of m. 28, beat 4 ____. Do these two chords resolve in the traditional manner? _____ .

3.   Are the diminished seventh chords in m. 26 and m. 29 spelled according to the way they function? _____ . Are these embellishing or functional diminished seventh chords? _____ .

4.   What pattern of key relationships is established in the "Tempo I" section? _____

CHAPTER TWENTY-FIVE

Binary and Ternary Forms

1. THREE WAYS OF LOOKING AT FORM

1A. In the work that follows:

1. Locate by beginning and ending measure numbers an example of each and explain your choice.

   • a pre-cadential extension _____

   reason? _____

   • a post-cadential extension _____

   reason? _____

   • a thematic passage _____

   reason? _____

2. Where do you first expect a cadence to occur? _____

   Why? _____

3. Where does the cadence you expect actually occur? ___

   What change(s) follow(s) it? _____

4. Provide harmonic analysis of mm. 17–22.

5. Discuss mm. 17–22 from the standpoint of sequence.

6. Measures 17–22 are a clear example of the transitional process. Explain why.

7. What process follows mm. 17–22? _____

Mozart: Piano Sonata K. 280 (first movement) 🔊

1B. Two musical processes are evident in the following passage. Locate and identify them, and cite features of the processes that you observe.

Beethoven: Sonata op. 2, no. 3 (third movement) 🔊

1C. For the two musical examples that follow:

1. Place the letters **R** (repeat), **V** (vary), or **C** (create) at each point where the composer made one of these decisions. (This is likely to be every measure or so.) If **R** or **V**, give the measure number of the source of the repetition or variation.

2. Identify the musical processes (thematic, transitional, developmental, cadential, or preparatory) present.

3. Each excerpt consists of approximately fifty beats of music. Which excerpt involves the greater number of musical processes? Does the number of processes present influence the character of each excerpt? If so, in what ways?

1   Beethoven: Piano Sonata op. 14, no. 2

2   Tchaikovsky: 18 Pieces, op. 72, no. 5 ("Meditation")

2. STATEMENT AND CONTRAST: BINARY AND TERNARY FORMS

2A. The four compositions that follow are organized according to date of composition, not according to degree of difficulty or form. Name and diagram the form of each. Then, answer additional questions as assigned by your instructor.

1   **J. S. Bach: French Suite no. 6, BWV 817 (Sarabande)** 🔊))

Bach composed the six French Suites at Cöthen between 1717 and 1723. The Sarabande, a triple meter "walking" dance with an exaggerated second step (beat), appears as the third movement in these suites.

1.   Diagram the form and name it. Include sections, phrases, and tonal changes, and measure numbers in your diagram.

2.   Which phrases form periods? Why?

3.   By what means is unity achieved? Variety?

4.   Locate and identify the important cadences.

5.   Locate and identify by Roman numeral five secondary functions:

   m.___: Key___: _____

   m.___: Key___: _____

   m.___: Key___: _____

   m.___: Key___: _____

   m.___: Key___: _____

J. S. Bach: French Suite no. 6, BWV 817 (Sarabande)

2   **Beethoven: Piano Sonata op. 26 (first movement)** 🔊

The Piano Sonata op. 26, written in 1802, begins in an unusual way–with a theme-and-variations. In doing this, Beethoven displayed a penchant for the unexpected that remained a life-long trait. The theme is given below.

1.   Diagram the form and name it. Include sections, phrases, and tonal changes, and measure numbers in your diagram.

2.   Which phrases form periods? Why?

3.   Locate and describe a phrase extension.

4.   Locate and describe a sequence.

5.   Locate and identify by Roman numeral five tonicizations:

   m.__: Key___: ____

   m.__: Key___: ____

   m.__: Key___: ____

   m.__: Key___: ____

   m.__: Key___: ____

2   Beethoven: Piano Sonata op. 26 (first movement) 🔊

3 Chopin: Mazurka op. 17, no. 2 🔊

In the Polish mazurka, Chopin found a source of musical inspiration. His 51 works with that title are refinements of the triple-meter dance that capture some of its characteristics. Among these are strong accents on the second or third beat and pedal points emulating bagpipe drones.

1. Diagram the form and name it. Include sections, phrases, and tonal changes, and measure numbers in your diagram.

2. The cadential process occurs somewhere within mm. 52–68. Locate it, and identify it as pre-cadential (approaching the cadence) or post-cadential (following the cadence).

3. List the musical elements responsible for the sectional contrast in this work.

4. Locate an example of the transitional process.

5. What purpose might the dynamic accents serve?

6. What chord is prolonged in mm. 39–49?

4   Liszt: "Il Pensieroso" (from *Annees de Pelerinage, Bk. II*) 🔊

Franz Liszt was an Austrian-born Hungarian who spoke French. Cosmopolitan by birth and upbringing, he traveled extensively and documented his sojourns by writing musical "souvenirs." Inspired by the sculpture, "The Thinker," he prefaced the work with these lines of Michelangelo:

> "I am thankful to sleep, and even more that I am made of stone, while injustice and shame still exist. My great fortune is not to see, not to feel; so do not wake me–speak softly."

1.   Diagram the form and name it. Include sections, phrases, tonal changes, and measure numbers in your diagram.

2.   Each of the three opening phrases comes to a cadence in a different tonality. What are they, and how are they related.

3.   Provide a harmonic analysis of mm. 33–39.

4.   The Neapolitan chord occurs prominently at two important points in the music. Locate them. Explain how the treatment of the chord breaks from earlier tradition.

5.   The piece ends with both pre-cadential and post-cadential extensions. Where are these? What term could be applied to the post-cadential extension? Locate a transitional passage.

2B. 1. Diagram the form and name it. Include sections (upper case letters), phrases (lower case letters), and tonal changes in your diagram. Locate everything by measure number.

2. Two motives help to unify this movement. Identify them.

3. What is the principal tonality of the movement? Is it reflected by the key signature?

4. Locate the earliest reference to a new tonality. Is this a modulation or tonicization?

5. What peculiarity is present at each cadence?

6. Identify the tonality at the beginning and end of the second section. Locate and describe a tonicization within this section.

1 Corelli: Trio Sonata op. 4, no. 3 (Sarabande) 🔊

2   Schubert: Impromptu op. 142, no.3 🔊

Provide a complete harmonic and formal analysis.

CHAPTER TWENTY-SIX

Introduction to Sonata Form

A. Listen to the movement that follows several times. As you do so, try to hear the various types of music in it–thematic, transitional, developmental, and cadential. Then answer these questions.

Form

1. The exposition ends in m.___. There is___ is not___ a transition to the secondary key.

2. The key of the second thematic/tonal area is ___. This key is, with respect to the home key, the: dominant___ the relative major___ other___.

3. The exposition ends with a cadential passage called a codetta. This passage begins at m. ___.

4. The development begins in m. ___. It focuses on material from the: first thematic/tonal area ___ second thematic/tonal area ___ closing area ___. A retransition occurs at m. ___, alluding to these tonalities: ___, ___, and ___.

5. The recapitulation begins in m. ___ in the key of ___.

6. In the recapitulation, the second thematic/tonal area begins in m. ___ in the key of ___. This key is, with respect to the home key, the: dominant ___ the relative major ___ other ___.

7. A coda begins in m. ___ in the key of ___. What is unusual about this coda? _____

Other Questions

1. The phrase/period structure of mm. 1–8 is:

    a a' (period) ___ a a' (no period) ___ a b (period) ___ a b (no period) ___

2. Fermatas occur at three points. What two musical processes does each fermata separate (thematic, transitional, developmental, cadential)?

    m. 16 _____

    m. 73 _____

    m. 106 _____

    m. 113 _____

3. A passage based entirely upon the sequential treatment of a motive occurs between m. ___ and m. ___. This process is _____ (thematic, cadential, developmental, transitional).

4. Identify by Roman numeral the following harmonies:

    m. 3, beat 1 ___

    m. 37, beat 2 ___

    m. 38, beat 4 ___

    m. 41, beat 4 ___

Beethoven: Piano Sonata op. 10, no. 1 (third movement)

B. Listen to the movement that follows several times. As you do so, try to hear the various types of music in it–thematic, transitional, developmental, and cadential. Then answer these questions.

Form

1. The exposition ends in m.___ . There is ___ is not ___ a transition to the secondary key.

2. The key of the second thematic/tonal area is ___. This key is, with respect to the home key, the: dominant ___ the relative major ___ other ___ .

3. The exposition ends with a cadential passage that might be called a codetta or a closing theme. This passage begins at m. ___ .

4. The development begins at m. 32 and consists of two subsections. The first, at m. 32, begins in ___ (key?) and derives material from ___ (what measures?). The second subsection begins at m. ___ in the key of ___ and derives material from ____ (what measures?).

5. A very brief retransition occurs at m. ___ .

6. The recapitulation begins in m. ___ in the key of ___ .

7. In the recapitulation, the second thematic/tonal area begins in m. ___ in the key of ___ . This key is, with respect to the home key, the: dominant ___ the relative minor ___ other ___ .

8. A coda is ____ is not ___ present.

Other Questions:

1. The music at mm. 58–63 is_____ (thematic, cadential, developmental, transitional).

2. The most remote tonal region of the movement occurs in m. ___. The key suggested at this point is ____ .

3. List the developmental techniques employed in the development section and give measure numbers: _____
_____ .

Mozart: Piano Sonata K. 330 (second movement) 🔊

CHAPTER TWENTY-SEVEN

Introduction to the Rondo

A.   Listen carefully several times to the rondo movement that follows. Then answer these questions.

Form

1.   The form of the refrain is: binary ___ rounded binary ___ ternary ___.

2.   The first episode begins in m. ___ in the key of ___. This key, with respect to the home tonality, is: the relative minor ___ the dominant ___ the parallel minor ___ other___. The refrain then modulates to ___.

3.   The form of the first episode is: binary ___ rounded binary ___ ternary ___.

4.   The second refrain begins at m. ___. It is a (an) exact___ varied___ repetition of the original.

5.   The second episode begins at m. ___ in the key of ___. This key, with respect to the home key, is: the dominant ___ the relative minor ___ the parallel minor ___ other ___.

6.   The final refrain begins in m. ___. In what ways does it differ from the previous two?

7.   The transitional process is evident in mm. ___—___.

8.   Of these processes–thematic, transitional, cadential–which is *least* in evidence?

Other

Locate an example of each:

Viio/V ___

V/ii ___

Deceptive cadence ___

V7/IV ___

V7/V ___

viio/vi ___

Haydn: Piano Sonata H XVI:37 (third movement)

B.   Listen carefully several times to the rondo movement that follows. Then answer these questions. NOTE: MM. 171–199 are a long, in-tempo cadenza that is an added formal feature in this movement.

1.   The refrain begins at m. 1 and ends in m. ___ .

2.   The first episode begins at m. ___ in the key of ___. A transition to this episode is___ is not ___ present.

3.   The refrain appears three more times: at m.___ , m. ___ , and m. ___ .

4.   A retransition precedes these reappearances of the refrain. These retransitions begin at m. ___ , m. ___ , and m. ___ .

5.   The longest and most complex episode (C) of the movement begins at m. 65 in the key of ___ . This episode contains three subsections that differ in tonality, musical material, and texture. The first subsection, at m. 65, is followed by a second at m. ___ , in the key of ___ , and a third at m. ___ that begins in the key of ___ .

6.   Which of the subsections in the C episode develops material from the refrain? ____ (give beginning measure number).

7.   Which refrain (1, 2, 3 or 4) is followed by a coda? ___ Where does this coda begin? ___ .

8.   This is a ___ five-part rondo ___seven-part rondo.

9.   One example of a cadential extension occurs at m. ___ .

10. The key at m. 95 is ___. In this key, how would you symbolize the tonicization in m. 99? _____ m. 100? _____ How would you symbolize the chord of m. 102? _____

     Give a diagram of this movement's form similar to that given for the Beethoven rondo

Diagram here:

Mozart: Piano Sonata K. 333 (third movement) 🔊

CHAPTER TWENTY-EIGHT

Syntax and Vocabulary

1. SYNTAX

1A. Construct examples of planing, using first-inversion triads. The first chord is given.

1   Chromatic planing beneath the melody

2   Diatonic planing beneath the melody: G major

3   Chromatic planing above the bass: dominant thirteenth chords in the given voicing.

1B. On separate manuscript paper, transform the following melodies into the indicated modes.

1   Change to: 1) Mixolydian 2) Lydian

2   Change to: 1) Aeolian 2) Dorian

3   Change to: 1) Phrygian 2) Mixolydian

1C. Identify the type of planing (diatonic or chromatic) and describe the harmonic structures and tonality or modality involved.

1   Debussy: "Soiree dans Grenade" (no. 2 from *Estampes*) 🔊

2   Debussy: "Les sons et les parfums tournent dans l'air du soir" (*Preludes*, Bk. I, no. 4) 🔊

3 Gershwin: "An American in Paris"

4   Debussy: Sonata for Flute, Viola, and Harp (Pastorale) 🔊

1D. Identify the mode implied by the following cadences.

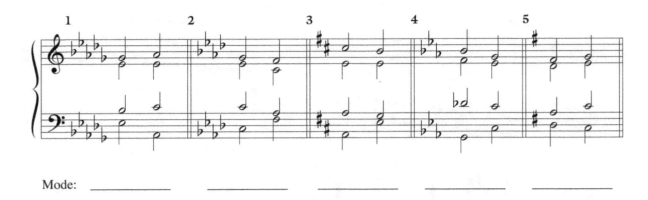

Mode: _____   _____   _____   _____   _____

1E. Illustrate in four voices cadences that suggest the following modes. Regard the given pitch as the final.

1F. The Sarabande from Debussy's suite, *Pour le Piano,* has been used to illustrate several techniques in this chapter. Answer these questions concerning the Sarabande, which appears complete following the questions.

Form

1. Describe the work's form. What elements define it?

2. Which of these processes–thematic, transitional, developmental, or cadential–are present? Give examples.

3. For mm. 1–22, label each two-measure gesture with a **C**, **R**, or **V** to indicate which compositional choice (**C**reate, **R**epeat, or **V**ary) Debussy made at that moment.

Syntax

1. Make functional sense of the harmonic syntax in mm. 50–55.

2. Locate additional examples of planing and mode use.

Debussy: *Pour le Piano* (Sarabande)

2. NEW MELODIC AND HARMONIC STRUCTURES

2A. Construct a major pentatonic or minor pentatonic scale on the given pitches.

1   Minor pentatonic on D

2   Minor pentatonic on F♯

3   Major pentatonic on A♭

4   Minor pentatonic on C♯

5   Major pentatonic on B♭

2B. These pitch collections can be arranged to form a complete pentatonic scale, whole tone scale, octatonic scale, or church mode. However, each collection contains one note that is *not* a member of the scale and one or more notes that should be respelled enharmonically. Eliminate pitch duplications, enharmonic spellings, and the pitch that does not belong and arrange the collections in ascending order to form one each of the scales. Then, identify the scale or mode.

1 _____

2 _____

3 _____

4 _____

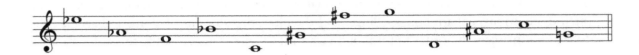

5 _____

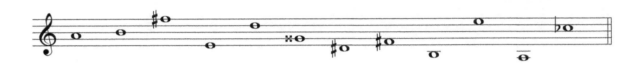

2C. Identify which of the following chords can be stacked as perfect fourths, and do so. Then, restack the same chord as a quintal harmony.

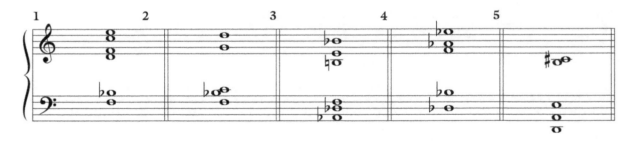

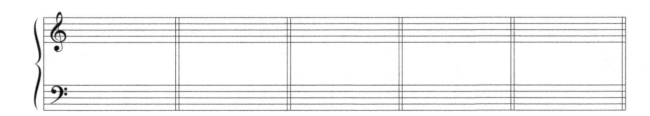

2D. Above each melody, write and identify the scale or mode on which it is based.

1 Write scale or mode:_____ Identify scale or mode:_____

2 Write scale or mode:_____ Identify scale or mode:_____

3 Write scale or mode:_____ Identify scale or mode:_____

4 Write scale or mode:_____ Identify scale or mode:_____

5 Write scale or mode:_____ Identify scale or mode:_____

2E. Follow the instructions preceding each melody.

1   Parallel to the melody, add two lower voices that constitute the chromatic planing of quartal harmonies. The first two beats are completed for you.

2   Parallel to the melody, add two lower voices that constitute chromatic planing.

3   Parallel to the melody, add two lower voices that constitute diatonic planing in E♭ Mixolydian.

2F. Compose a short ABA′ form for solo piano or for your melody instrument with piano (or guitar) accompaniment using the techniques discussed in this chapter. Try to define the form through register, through the types of devices used in each section, and through cadences. Vary the return of the A material in some way. You might begin with a general verbal description of your intentions, such as this, which is tailored for a solo instrument with piano accompaniment:

A: Low-register melodic line in Dorian mode on E♭. Restate the line in the medium-high register, accompanied by mid-register diatonic planing of triads in the same mode. End with a Dorian cadence.

B: Medium-high register arpeggiations that imply fragments of the A melody over an extreme low-register pedal point in the piano. Lead without cadence into the A′.

A′: Restate the A melody in the medium-high register accompanied by chromatic planing of triads or quartal harmonies. Repeat the last several of these triads over and over while retating the A melody in the solo instrument and piano in the Dorian mode on E♭, ending with a Dorian cadence.

2G. Answer these questions concerning Debussy's "Des pas sur la neige:"

1. Describe the form. What principal unifying device does Debussy use?

2. A "falling third" motive occurs many times in the piece. Circle each appearance.

3. Identify the tonal center, and explain how it is created.

4. Locate and describe prominent examples of parallelism.

5. What mode is suggested in mm. 1–4?

6. Locate in mm. 1–13 several examples of major-minor seventh chords that do not function as dominant sevenths. (NOTE: Some may be disguised through enharmonic spelling.)

7. Analyze the chord of m. 14 in an appropriate way.

8. Identify the underlying harmonies in mm. 23–24.

9. What key or mode is suggested in m. 28 (last beat) through m. 31? (Consider the harmonic implications of the melody as well as those of the accompanying chords.)

10. Identify the cadence that ends the piece.

Debussy: "Des pas sur la neige" (Preludes, Book I , no. 6)

CHAPTER TWENTY-NINE
New Tonal Methods

1. NEW TONAL VENTURES

1A. Each of the harmonies listed appears once. Place the letter corresponding to the harmony in the appropriate blank. (Beware of enharmonic spellings and octave duplications.) Although quartal harmonies sound "rootless," a letter name is provided along with the symbol "Q" to indicate the pitch above which the chord is built.

a) A/F^Q

b) Q (4-note)

c) C#^{Q}

d) vi^{11}

e) A♭^{6}/E

f) B^Q/F

g) C^6/D♭

h) V^{13}

i) 11^9

j) A^Q

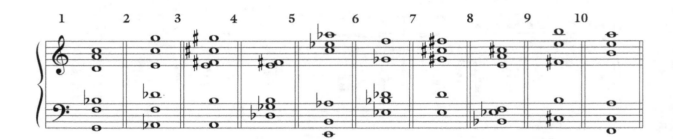

1B. Provide a symbol that accurately describes the following harmonic structures. Consider spacing when deciding whether to analyze a harmony as a polychord or a triadic extension. Consider the prevailing interval structure when deciding whether to analyze a harmony as quintal, quartal, or triadic.

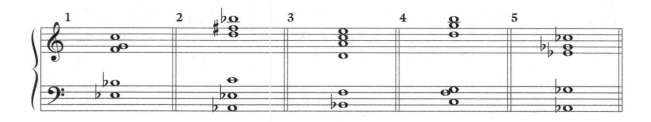

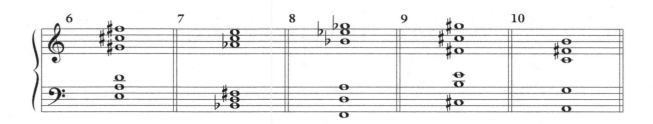

1C. Identify the following harmonies as quartal, a polychord, or a triadic extension, and symbolize each in an appropriate way.

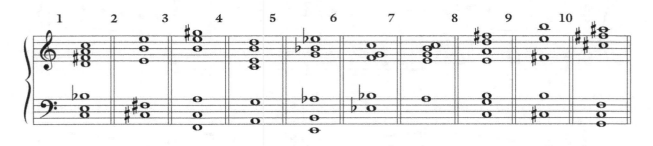

1D. Construct the specified harmony above the given bass.

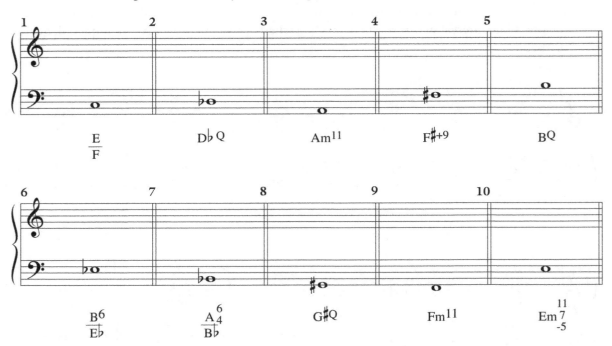

1E. Continue the three different accompaniments to the melodic line in the same style.

1   Bimodal (use a mode different from that of the melody but based on the same final) 🔊

2 Pandiatonic with counterlines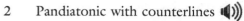

3 Polytonal

1F.   Each of the passages that follows employs one or more techniques discussed in Chapters 28 and 29. Identify the techniques. Choose one passage, and continue it for another four bars in the manner begun.

1

2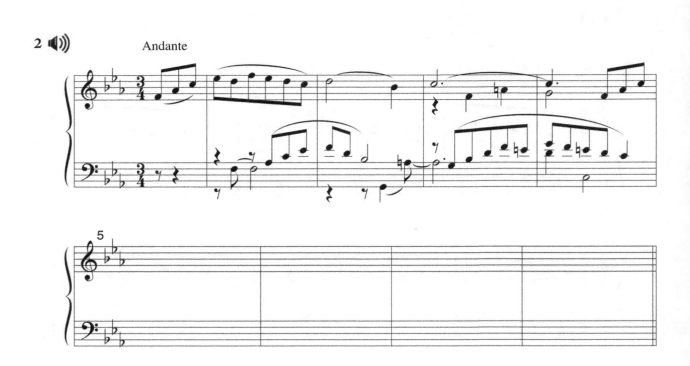

2. STRAVINSKY AND BARTÓK

2A. Answer the questions that follow each excerpt.

1   **Hindemith: Sonata for Flute and Piano (first movement)** 🔊

1.   What is the tonal center? How is it created?

2.   Point to some quartal and quintal structures outlined melodically.

3.   Scalar motion is prominent in Hindemith's melodic lines. Point to some examples. Do the lines appear to be based on a scale or mode? Explain.

2   Stravinsky: Le Sacre du Printemps (Part Two: "The Sacrifice") 🔊

1. What two tonal centers exist? Where and how is each created?

2. On what scale or mode does the melody in mm. 19–22 appear to be based?

3. Provide chord symbols that give the most meaningful description of the sustained chords.

4. Provide analysis of the eighth-note chords in the passage.

3   Bartók: Sixth Quartet (first movement) 🔊

1.   What do you hear as the tonal center in this passage? Why?

2.   Describe the relationship between the Violin I and Cello ostinatos. What pitch pattern do they create together? What is the scalar basis of this pattern?

3.   Describe the relationship between the Violin II and Viola parts.

4.   What happens to all the parts as this passage unfolds?

5.   Describe the harmonic structures formed by the four lines in combination.

2B.   Answer the questions that follow each excerpt.

1   **Stravinsky: Symphony of Psalms (first movement)** 🔊

1.   What pitch is established as a tonic? How?

2.   Describe the harmonic basis of the passage.

2   Mario Castelnuevo-Tedesco: *Platero y Yo*, op. 190 (vol. I, no. 2 "Angelus")

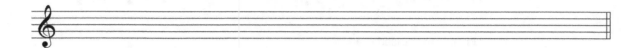

1.   In what key does the music begin? In what key does it end?

2.   Describe the harmonic relationships present.

3.   What evidence of harmonic function can you find?

4.   Beyond harmonic function, how is a tonic established?

5.   Identify and describe examples of planing and sequence.

3   Bartók: "Song of the Harvest" (from *Forty-Four Violin Duets*) 🔊

Note: Guitar sounds an octave lower than written.

1. Describe the pitch content of each violin part. What is the result of the two parts in combination?

2. How are mm. 16–20 related to mm. 1–5? How are mm. 6–14 related to mm. 21–29?

3. What is unique about mm. 30–33?

4. Identify prominent contrapuntal techniques.

5. Describe the form, using letter names to show sections and their relationships.

CHAPTER THIRTY
Atonality and Serialism

1. ATONALITY

1A. Identify the interval class of each.

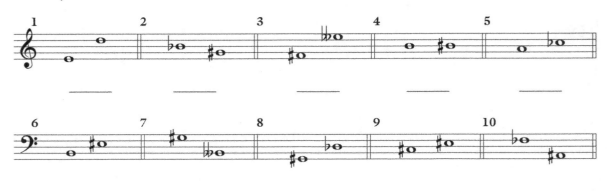

1B. Using the given pitch, notate five different intervals that produce the same interval class. Feel free to use enharmonic spellings of the given pitch.

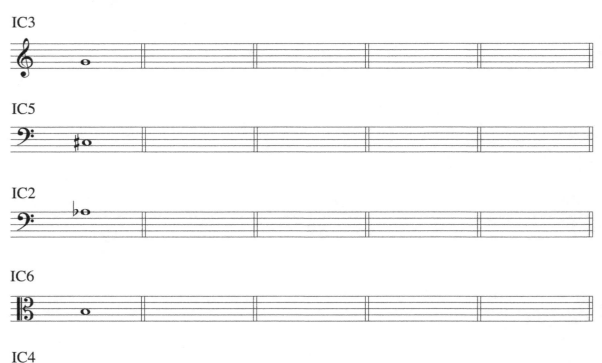

1C. Place the following pitch collections in normal order, and give the set type. Observe the clefs.

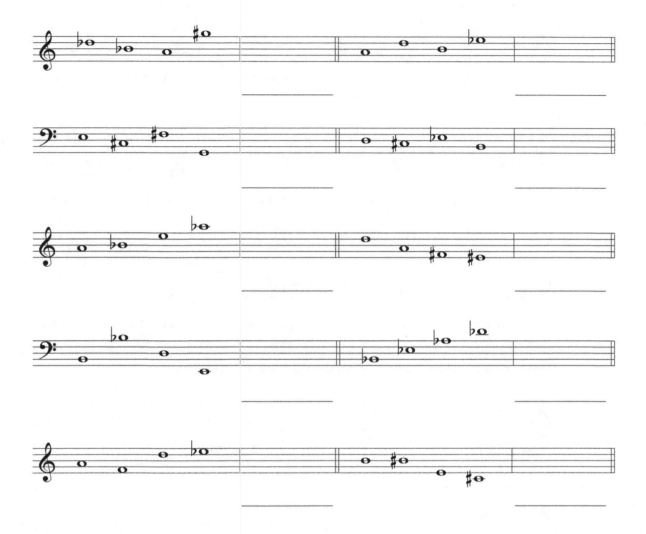

1D. Construct the specified sets using the given pitch as the starting note.

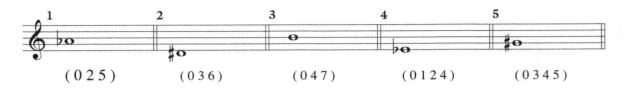

(025)   (036)   (047)   (0124)   (0345)

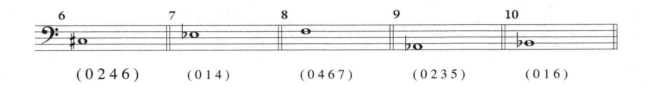

(0246)   (014)   (0467)   (0235)   (016)

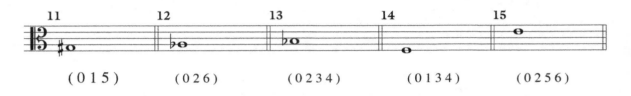

(015)   (026)   (0234)   (0134)   (0256)

1E. Construct the specified sets. Next to each set, show its inversion.

1 Set (02356)   2 Set (0134)

3 Set (034)   4 Set (0247)

5 Set (0146)   6 Set (025)

7 Set (0267)   8 Set (03467)

9 Set (0136)   10 Set (0347)

1F. Arrange each ordered set in normal order and give its numeric description beneath. Then show the inversion, using the last note of the normal order as the first note of the inversion. Finally, arrange the set in best normal order and show its prime form (set type).

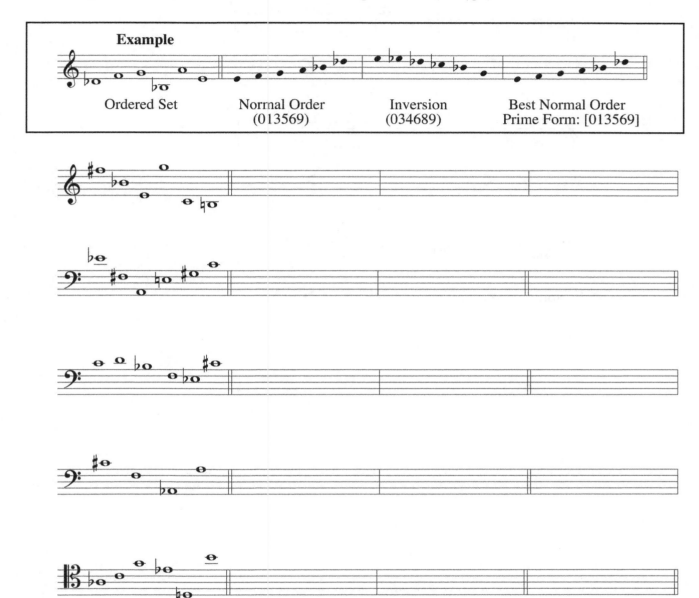

1G. Create an interval vector for the following sets.

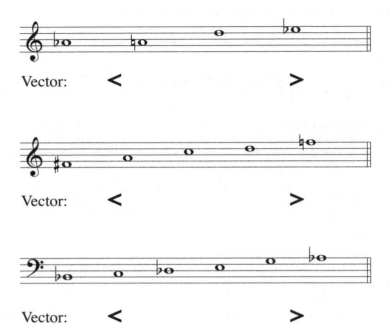

Vector: <   >

Vector: <   >

Vector: <   >

1H. Answer the following questions concerning Schoenberg's *Klavierstücke*. The first four measures appear in the textbook on page 528. Refer to this page to answer the following questions regarding the example below.)

1. Locate additional appearances of the set that opens this movement (see textbook page 528).

2. The set identified in the opening measures is not the only one used in this work. Identify one other set that appears more than once.

3. Explain how measures 17–24 could be viewed as a single phrase or a phrase group.

Suggestion:

Listen to this work several times before undertaking analysis. Many relationships that are not readily apparent to the eye are often revealed through careful listening, and vice versa.

Schoenberg: *Klavierstücke*, op. 11, no. 1

11. The excerpt that follows was composed by Anton Webern (1883–1945). Schoenberg's most
     illustrious student brought extreme harmonic unity and economy of means to the atonal style.
     Determine the set that is responsible for the harmonic unity in the passage that follows, and
     show examples.

Webern: *Fünf Sätze für Streichquartett* (third movement) 🔊

1J. Listen carefully to Daniel McCarthy's "The Drums of Moria" from *Time Out of Mind: Six Tales of Middle Earth*, a work based on Tolkien's trilogy, *The Lord of the Rings*. Then answer the following questions: 🔊

 1. Identify the harmonic unit on which the excerpt is based. To what other harmonic system does it relate?

 2. How many phrases do you hear? What tells you a phrase has ended? What logical pattern of development do you hear in the succession of phrases?

 3. Describe the relationship between: m. 113 and m. 116; m. 113 and m. 121

 4. Aside from the relationships you noted in answer to question 3, what other measures in this excerpt are related? Describe the relationship.

Daniel McCarthy: "The Drums of Moria" (from *Time Out of Mind: Six Tales of Middle Earth*)

2. SERIALISM

2A. Provide the indicated transformations of the following row: P9, R7, I5, and RI3. The first pitch is given for each.

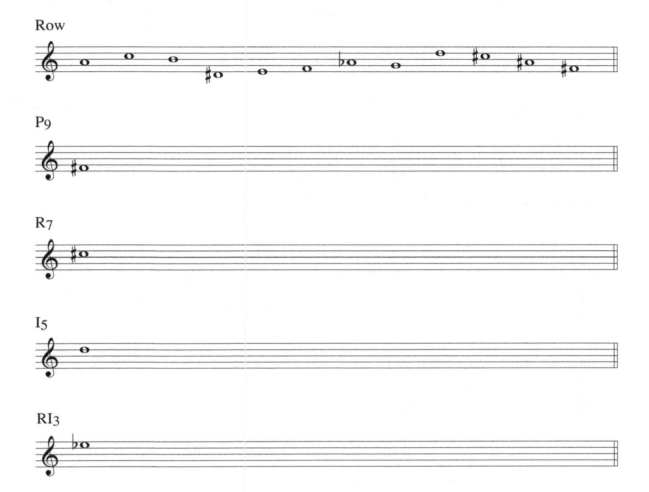

Row

P9

R7

I5

RI3

2B. A 12-tone row follows, along with the beginnings of four transformations. Identify and complete each transformation.

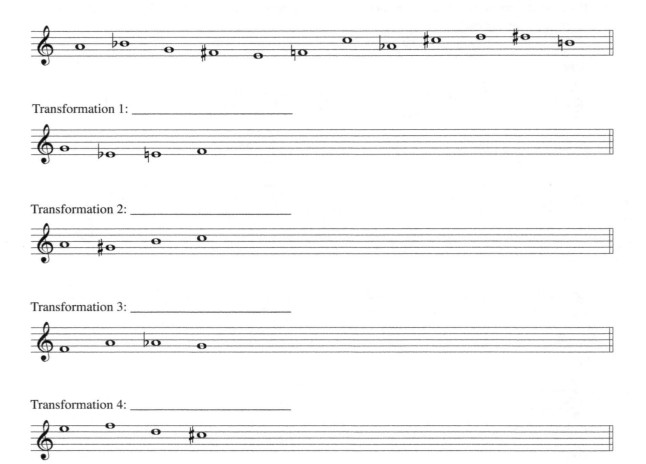

Transformation 1: _____

Transformation 2: _____

Transformation 3: _____

Transformation 4: _____

2C. The two rows that follow are quite different, reflecting each composer's musical goals. Analyze and compare their structures. Then complete a matrix for the second row.

1   **Webern: Row from String Quartet op. 28**

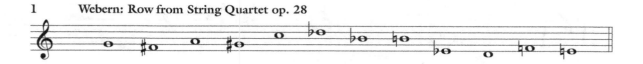

2   **Dallapiccola: Row from *Goethe Songs* (No. 1)**

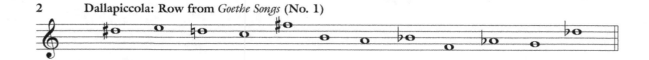

2D. Answer the questions that follow concerning Schoenberg's *Klavierstücke*, op. 33a.

1.   How many pitch classes are present in m. 1? In m. 2?

2.   How do the following chords in mm. 1–2 relate to each other?

Chords 1 and 6?

Chords 2 and 5?

Chords 3 and 4?

3.   Based on your answers to the preceding questions, what deductions can you make concerning the row forms employed in the first two measures?

4.   In m. 3–5, locate melodic statements that correspond to the first six chords. Circle these on the music and label them "Chord 1," "Chord 2," and so on.

5.   Using all the information gathered in answer to the preceding questions, construct the P0 form of the row. Then, construct the other row form used in these five measures and identify it.

6.   Complete the row analysis through m. 11.

7.   Explain how mm. 10–11 relate to mm. 1–2.

8.   What property of the row permits Schoenberg to use two forms simultaneously without duplicating pitches?

Schoenberg: *Klavierstücke*, op. 33a

2E. Using one of the rows given in this chapter or one of your own creation, compose a 16- to 24-measure piece for any two melodic instruments (for example, flute and oboe, or trumpet and trombone). Incorporate some of the techniques discussed in the chapter. You may first want to create an outline of your piece, such as the one suggested here.

First eight measures:

	Legato melody: high register			Legato accompaniment in longer notes values: low register
Flute:	P_0	P_3	RI_0	

	Legato accompaniment in longer notes values: mid register			Legato melody: high register
Oboe:	I_0	R_3	R_0	
				Retrograde of flute part, but not necessarily a rhythmic retrograde

Second eight measures:

More animated, shorter note values

Flute:	R_0	R_3	P_0	P_3

Oboe:	I_0	Repeated four-note fragment from I9 as ostinato

CHAPTER THIRTY-ONE

Harmonic Principles in Jazz

1. EXTENDING THE TRIAD

1A. Give the symbol for the *basic* triad or seventh chord–D°7, Fm, Cm7, Gm7–5, and so on (see p. 556)—that has been extended or altered. Do not show the extensions or alterations. All chords are in root position.

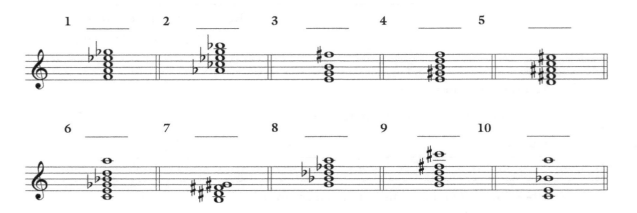

1B. Using Example 31-2 in your text as a guide, place in the first blank a chord symbol that precisely describes each harmony (all are in root position). NOTE: More than one way of expressing these chords exists.

In the second blank, indicate which seventh chord–MM7, Mm7, mM7, mm7, om7, or oo7–forms the basis for the extended harmony.

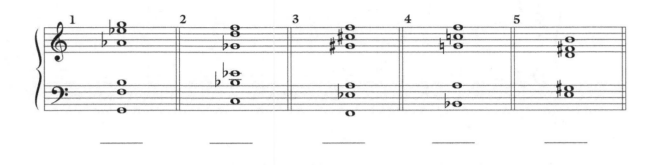

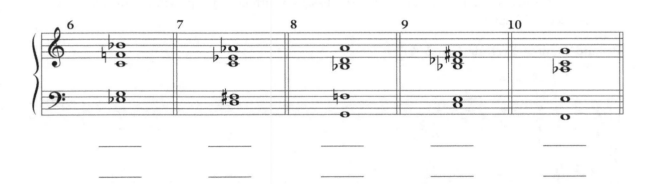

1C. Write these chords in root-position unvoiced form. For guidance, refer to Example 31-2 and the seven points that follow it.

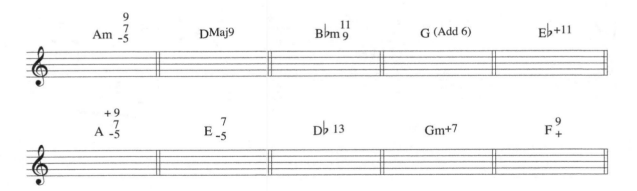

1D. Beneath the melodic line, show an extended version of the given basic seventh chord that is compatible with each melody pitch. Do not voice the chord. Simply stack it in thirds. Use both staves if needed. If the extended chord member duplicates the melody pitch, name it in the blank beneath the music (b9, #5, +11, and so on).

Chord member: ____   ____   ____   ____   ____   ____   ____

1E. Place the extended chord symbol in the first blank and the basic seventh chord symbol in the second blank. In some measures, only the basic seventh chord is present. If so, place an X in the second blank.

Roland Hanna: Prelude No. 2 🔊))

1F. The chords that follow are voiced according to either Template 1 or Template 2 (see pages 562–563 in your text). Identify the template used (1 or 2). Then, revoice the chord using the other template.

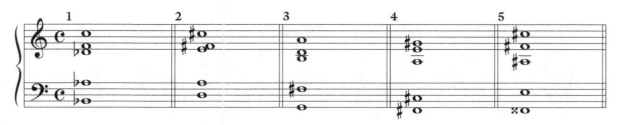

Template: _____   _____   _____   _____   _____

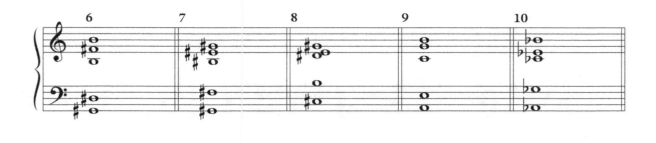

_____   _____   _____   _____   _____

1G. Give the basic chord symbol in the upper blank and, where a further extension is present, the more complete symbol in the lower blank. The first measure is completed for you. Where a chord's identity is problematic, remember that an extension or alteration might be spelled enharmonically.

1   **Toots Thielemans: "Bluesette"** 🔊

Basic symbol: G   _____   _____   _____

Extended symbol: Gadd9   _____   _____   _____

_____   _____   _____   _____

2   Bill Evans: "Turn out the Stars"

* The G is an enharmonically spelled ♯5 (F𝄪).

2.   CHORD SUBSTITUTION

2A. Voice the first chord in each measure. Use a voicing that creates smooth voice leading into the second chord. Then add Roman numerals that symbolize the tonicizing chord groups (ii-V patterns).

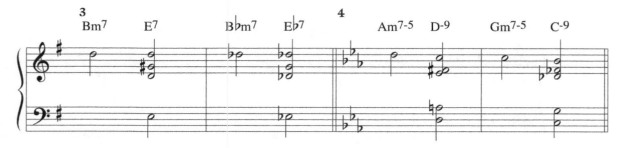

2B. Complete each sequence of ii-V patterns at the pitch level suggested by the melody notes. Provide lead-sheet symbols above the chords and functional analysis beneath, as begun. The final chord is the dominant or its substitute.

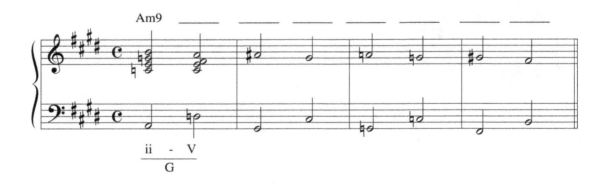

2C. Notate the tritone-related dominant seventh chord for the following:

2D. In the second measure, turn the given chord into a V7–5. If the chord is already a V7–5, leave the second measure empty. Then, in the third measure, write the V7–5 that can be substituted for the given chord.

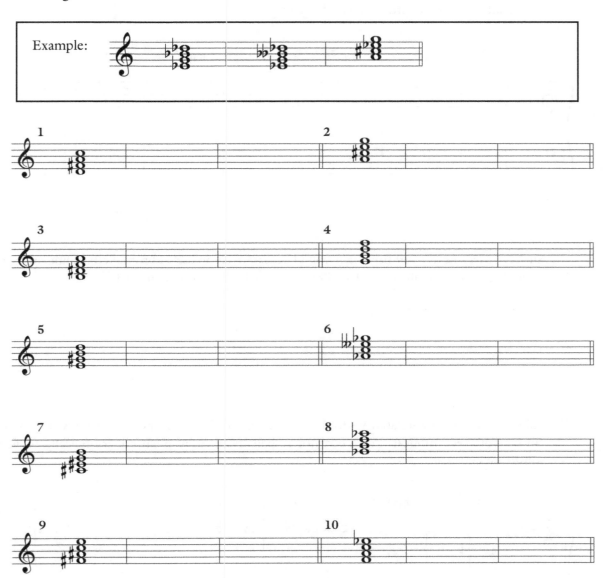

2E. 1   Create a chromatic chord progression by substituting tritone-related dominants for the given dominant seventh chords where possible. Place the chord symbols for these substitutes in the appropriate blanks. Then voice the new chord pattern on the grand staff. The first chord is voiced for you.

Bm7-5   E7   Am7-5   D7   Gm7-5   C7   F

2   Show the tritone substitutions that will (1) create a completely chromatic bass line ending on G, and (2) create a chromatic bass line ending with a leap to G from D.

F7   Bb7   Eb7   Ab7   G

1)   __   __   __   __   __

2)   __   __   __   __   __

2F.   Substitute the tritone-related V7 for the second chord (boxed). Then resolve it with a minimal amount of voice motion. You need not respell the melody pitch enharmonically to fit the substitute chord.

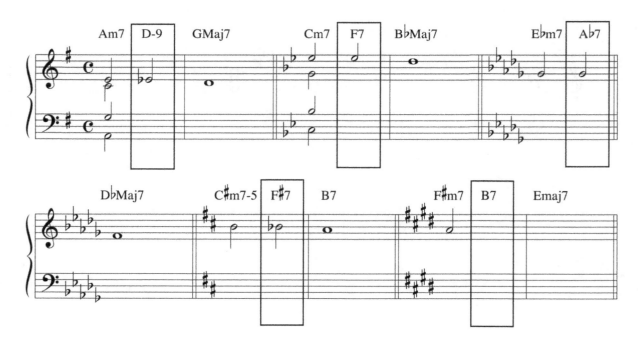

2G. Answer the questions concerning the following excerpts.

1   **Bill Evans: "Orbit"**

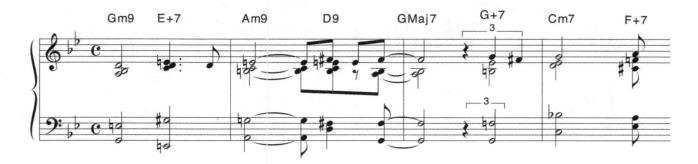

1.   Locate and label all tonicizing chords (V7) and mark tonicizing chord groups (ii7-V7).

2.   Identify all harmonic sequences. At what pitch level do these sequences repeat?

3.   The chord symbols in this published version are not always complete. What symbols would account for *all* the pitches in the chords at: m. 2, beat 3___; m. 3, beat 1___; m. 4, beat 1___?

2   Heyward, Gershwin, and Gershwin: "I Loves You, Porgy" (from *Porgy and Bess*) 🔊

1. Add lead-sheet symbols in the blanks above the chords.

2. Working backward from the tonicized BbMaj7 of m. 3, explain how the chords of m. 1 have been obtained. (HINT: First consider tonicization, then consider tritone substitution of dominants.)

3. The chord at the end of m. 4 is a tritone substitute for _____ (what secondary dominant?).
    The chord at the end of m. 5 is a tritone substitute for _____ (what secondary dominant?).

3.   IMPLIED LINES

3A.   Create a counterline based on the given harmonies and notate the line against the melody on the extra staff. Remember that each of the chord alterations has a potential implication for an implied line.

1   **Betty Comden, Adolph Green, and Jule Styne: "Make Someone Happy" (as performed by Bill Evans, LP: Verve V6 8803)**

2   **Otto Harbach and Jerome Kern: "Yesterdays" Arr. R.T.**

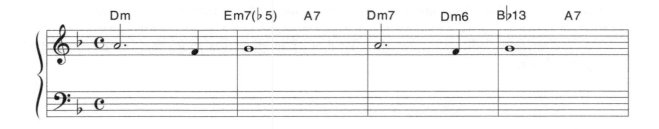

3B. Notate the implied bass line. One other ascending scalar line is embedded in the chord scheme. Notate it as well on the lower staff.

B.G. DeSylva, Lew Brown, and Ray Henderson: "The Birth of the Blues"

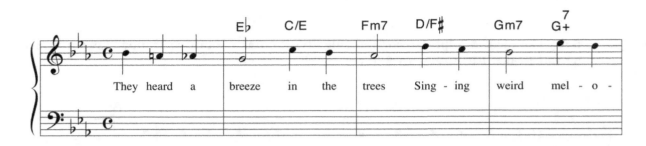

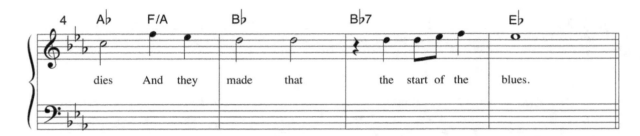

3C. Provide harmonic analysis.

Andre Previn: "In Our Little Boat" 🔊

1. On the blank staff following the music, notate the implied scalar line in mm. 38–42.

2. In the blanks above the music, add lead-sheet symbols that reflect the complete chords.

3. At the asterisks, indicate by lead-sheet symbol an appoggiatura chord that could replace the given chord.

Andre Previn: "In Our Little Boat"

Notate implied line here:

CHAPTER THIRTY-TWO

The Blues

1. BLUES FORM AND HARMONIC PRACTICE

1A. Identify the key of each blues pattern. Using as a guide the basic blues pattern of Example 32-2 from your text, notate the missing harmonies in the empty measures. In the blanks, provide lead-sheet symbols to show the additions or changes to the basic pattern that are suggested.

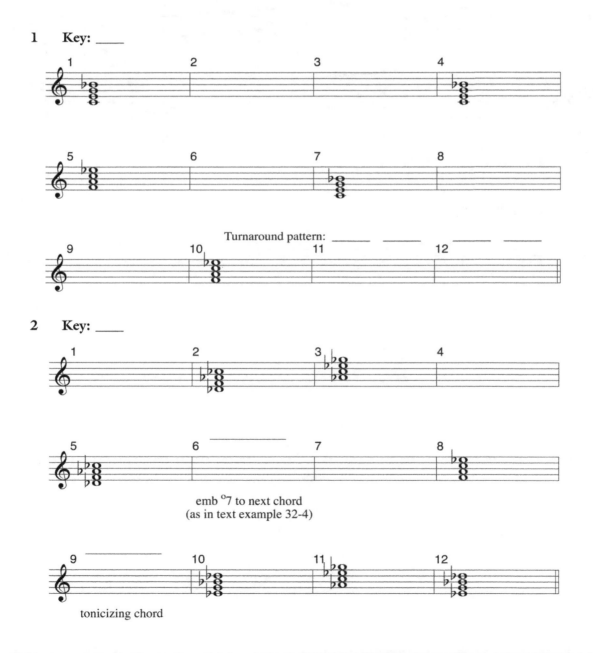

1   Key: ____

Turnaround pattern: ____ ____   ____ ____

2   Key: ____

____

emb °7 to next chord
(as in text example 32-4)

____

tonicizing chord

3 Key: _____

Tonicizing chord

Tritone sub. for tonicizing chord

4 Key: _____

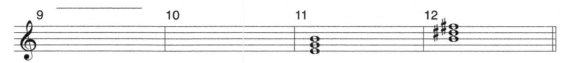

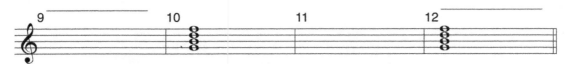

Tonicizing chord   Tritone substitute

1B. Write the twelve-bar blues changes given in Example 32-2, notating the unvoiced chords and showing the lead-sheet symbols above the chords. Be sure to place the chords in the correct location within the twelve-measure scheme.

1   In B♭:

2   In G:

3   **In E♭:**

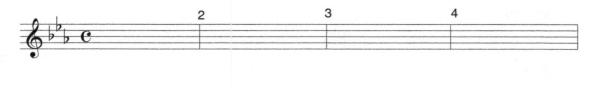

1C. Following are the first four measures of twelve-bar blues patterns. Identify and explain the harmonic substitutions.

1   G13 | C13 | G13 | Dm7 D♭9 |

2   B♭m6 | B13 | B♭m6 | B♭-9 |

3   B♭13 | E♭13 | B♭13 F♯m7 | Fm9 B♭-13 |

4   A♭13 D13 | D♭13 | A♭13 E9 | E♭9 D9 |

1D. Elaborate the patterns, notating all chords, and providing lead-sheet symbols.

1   (in A♭)

1.   In mm. 11–12, create a turnaround such that the chord roots descend chromatically to the I of m. 1.

2.   In m. 4, create a ii-V tonicization to precede the IV in m. 5.

3.   In mm. 9–10, replace the given chords with the tritone substitute for V7/V followed by V.

2   (in C minor)

1.   In mm. 11–12, create a turnaround such that the chord roots descend chromatically to the i of m. 1.

2.   In m. 4, create a ii-V tonicization to precede the IV in m. 5.

3.   In mm. 9–10, replace the iiø7 with the tritone-related dominant seventh leading to V in m. 10.

2. BLUES MELODIC PRACTICE AND BLUES VARIANTS

2A. Write the blue note scale shown in textbook Example 32-10 on the following pitches:

2B. Thelonius Monk's "Straight, No Chaser" is ingeniously constructed from a melodic motive. How does the melody relate to the blue note scale? Provide analysis above the music similar to the way you analyzed J. S. Bach's Inventions to show how the motive is manipulated. Be sure to comment on its rhythmic placement.

Thelonius Monk: "Straight, No Chaser"

2C. Create a 12-bar blues melody comprising only the blue note scale. Use Horace Silver's "Cookin' at the Continental" as a guide, but try to make your tune as different from that one as possible. Place appropriate lead-sheet chord symbols above the melody.

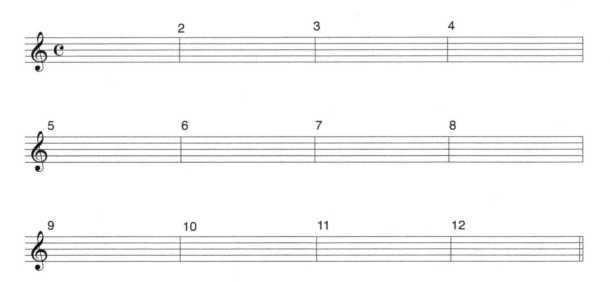

2D. Continue the melodic patterns for a full twelve measures, adhering to the a a′ b form illustrated
in Example 32-9 (see page 594 in your text). Optional: Add appropriate lead-sheet symbols
and/or continue the left-hand voicings of the first four measures.

2E. Compose for your instrument a twelve-bar blues with the melodic form a a′ b. The level of harmonic elaboration is up to you. Add lead-sheet symbols above the melody.

2F. Continue the following patterns through the entire twelve-bar harmonic structure of the blues. Optional: Create a pattern of your own and follow it through.

2

2G. 1. In what ways is this music similar to and different from the basic blues as presented in this chapter?

 2. Circle the blue notes present.

 3. How many phrases do you hear? How would you symbolize their relationships?

Ralph Turek: "Huz Bluz" 🔊

CHAPTER THIRTY-THREE

Shaping a Song

1. TEXT

1A. Select a meter, and then "rhythmize" one of the following texts, performing each of these steps:

1. Scan the text, placing accent marks on stressed syllables, adding breath marks at natural cadences, and underlining rhyming words.

2. Create a precisely notated rhythmic reading of the text that reflects your scansion.

3. Turn this rhythmic version of the text into an original melody, using melodic motives or sequences to correspond to repeated rhythms, varied repetitions of text, or parallel ideas.

Text a

"There is a season where heart-break's goin' 'round. There is a price you pay when you fool around. It's not a matter that we can talk about, it's just that I'm the one you can do without. And in the season when love is everywhere, I'm gonna find out that you just don't really care. It's not a matter that you will or you won't, you got the answer and don't you say you don't!" (Daniel McCarthy: "Hurting Season")

Text b

"You got me playin' funk in a minor mode ever since you left me standing here in the cold. When you left me, I was on my knees. Now I only write in minor keys. I tried to write it happy, in a major key. It took a lot tryin', it took a major part out of me." (Daniel McCarthy: "Funk in a Minor Mode")

2. COMPOSING A SONG STEP-BY-STEP

2A. Select one of the texts below, *or write one yourself.* Using the step-by-step method described in this chapter, set the lyrics to a minimum of sixteen measures of music. Texts a and c below are transformed into songs that you can hear (Workbook CD Tracks 200 and 201).

Text a

VERSE
"He said, 'She said I just want no one else but you.' Then she said, "He said she had heard that I was untrue.' Then she said to me, 'Oh, baby don't lie, cause if what I've heard is true, then I'm gonna cry.' He said, 'I've been lied to before.' And I said to her:

CHORUS
"'Life was so fine, when you were mine.' You said I lied, she saw me cry, I said, 'I love you.' You said 'Goodbye.' I asked you why? She said, 'I lied. My heart had died.' You said you loved me."

Daniel McCarthy: "He Said, She Said"

He Said, She Said

Words and Music by
Daniel McCarthy

Text b

VERSE

"So many times I have lost in love, in doesn't seem right. The pain and ache you're feeling now will turn to love again somehow. But darling when you reach out and hold me, I'm forgetting all the stories they told me."

CHORUS

"Because of love, I have walked the cutting edge of time. Because of love, I can never be the way I was before{.}"

Text c

CHORUS

"Jimmy remembers a time back when{.} But Jimmy knows he's in love again! Jimmy knows that its 'gonna grow. Never be lonely again! "

VERSE

"Singing alone at night, Singing with all his might. Feeling the blues can affect you, Tonight won't make it right. Talk on the Telephone. No darlin' to please come home. All he can do, is dream of you 'till night turns into day."

Daniel McCarthy: "Jimmy Knows" 🔊

Jimmy Knows

**Words and Music by
Daniel McCarthy**

Jim - my knows that it's go - nna grow,____ ne - ver be lone - ly a - gain!____

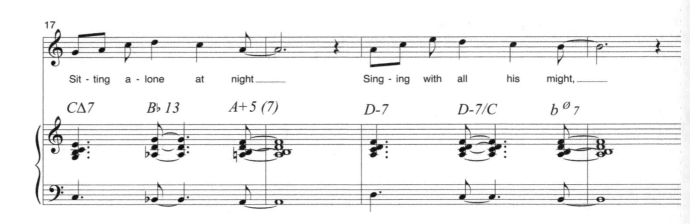

Sit - ting a - lone at night____ Sing - ing with all his might,____

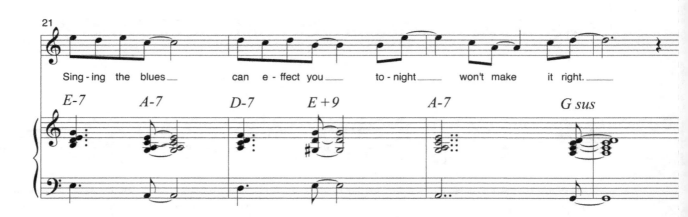

Sing - ing the blues____ can e - ffect you____ to - night____ won't make it right.____

APPENDIX A

Pitch

1. PITCH AND ITS NOTATION

1A. Before each note, add the clef (treble, bass, alto, or tenor) in which the pitch would be correctly named.

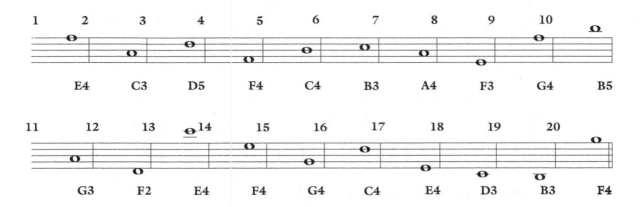

1B. In the blank beneath each pitch, write its letter name, using the correct octave designation. (Note the clef changes.)

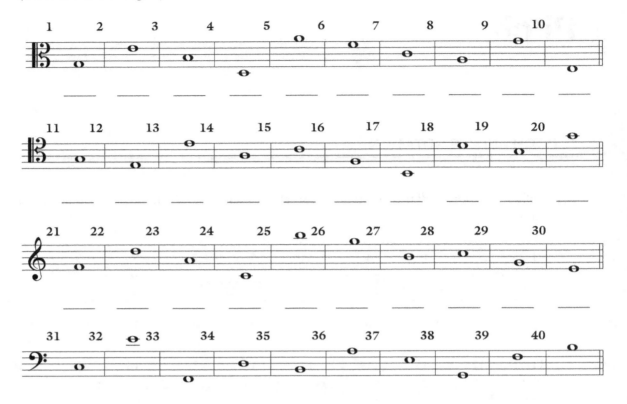

1C. Renotate the pitches in the clefs indicated.

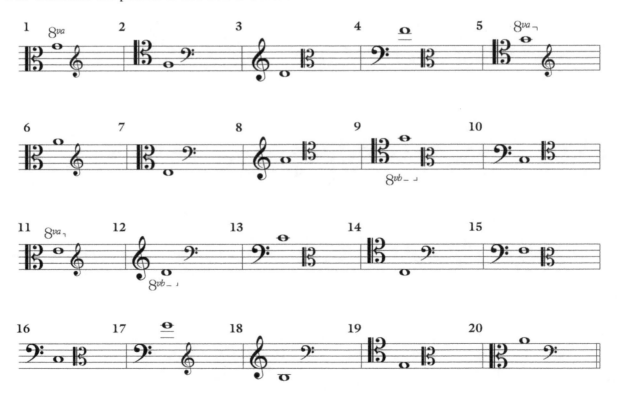

1D. Rewrite the following melody in bass clef.

1E. Renotate the following melodic phrases in the clef (treble, alto, tenor, or bass) requiring the fewest notes with ledger lines. If the given clef requires no greater number of notes with ledger lines than any of the other three possibilities, indicate this by writing *O.K.* on the blank staff.

1F. Indicate whether the interval is a half step (h) or whole step (w).

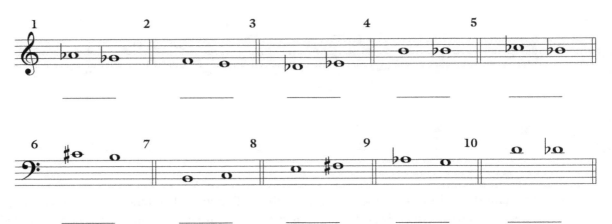

1G. Write a diatonic half step (h) or whole step (w) above or below the given pitch, as directed.

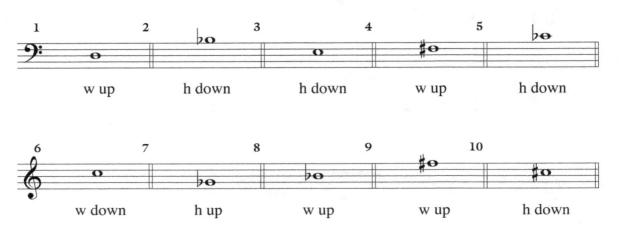

1H. Observing the clef sign, notate the pitch in the correct octave. Then write the diatonic half step above it.

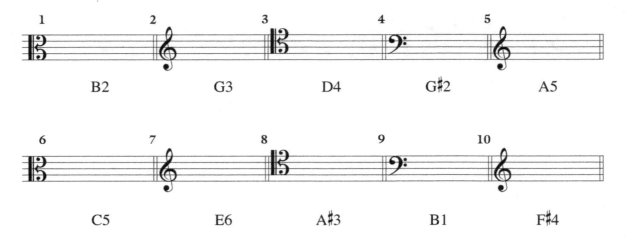

1I.   Match the enharmonic pitches.

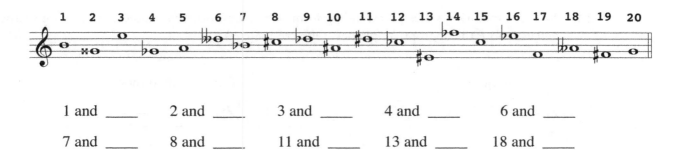

1 and ____   2 and ____   3 and ____   4 and ____   6 and ____

7 and ____   8 and ____   11 and ____   13 and ____   18 and ____

1J.   Place a check in the blank beneath each enharmonically equivalent pair of intervals.

2. SCALES AND KEYS

2A. Write the following scales (in ascending form only, unless otherwise indicated), placing sharps or flats before the appropriate pitches. Observe the clefs.

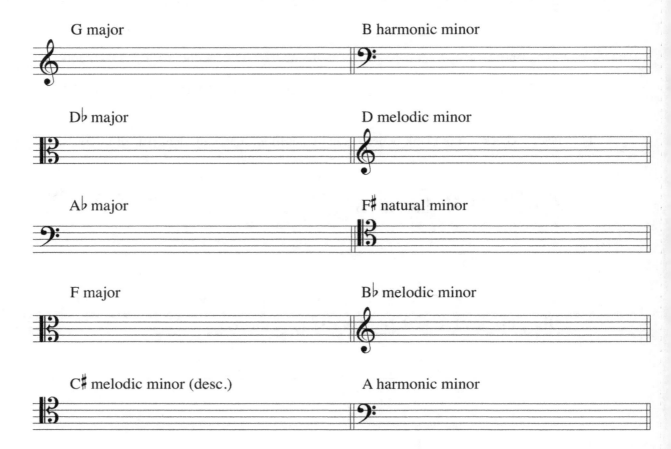

2B. Write the key signature for the following scales.

1   Relative major of B minor

2   Relative minor of G major

3   Parallel major of E♭ minor

4   Parallel minor of B♭ major

5   Relative major of C♯ minor

6   Relative minor of B major

7   Parallel major of A minor

8   Parallel minor of D major

9   Relative major of F minor

10   Relative minor of D♭ major

2C. Correct the errors in the following scales by changing, adding, or deleting accidentals. If no errors are present, indicate this with the notation "*O.K.*"

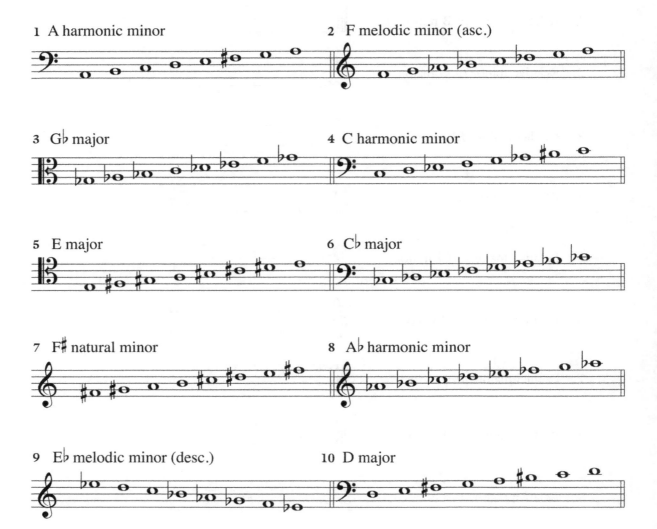

1 A harmonic minor

2 F melodic minor (asc.)

3 G♭ major

4 C harmonic minor

5 E major

6 C♭ major

7 F♯ natural minor

8 A♭ harmonic minor

9 E♭ melodic minor (desc.)

10 D major

2D. Name a scale—major or any minor scale form—in which each of the following appears:

1. as the upper tetrachord

2. as the lower tetrachord

If a pattern does not appear as the upper or lower tetrachord in any major or minor scale, place an X in the corresponding space. In some cases, *more* than two correct answers are possible.

1. _____ 1. _____ 1. _____ 1. _____ 1. _____

2. _____ 2. _____ 2. _____ 2. _____ 2. _____

1. _____ 1. _____ 1. _____ 1. _____ 1. _____

2. _____ 2. _____ 2. _____ 2. _____ 2. _____

2E. Identify the minor scale form used (assume the final pitch to be the tonic), and then notate the complete scale.

Scale form: _____

Scale form: _____

Scale form: _____

Scale form: _____

Scale form: _____

2F.   Transpose each melody as specified. Add the new key signature.

1   Beethoven: Piano Sonata, op. 2, no. 3 (first movement)

Transpose to D:

2   "Morris Dance" (England)

Transpose to F:

2G. After each melodic fragment, name and write the scale upon which it is based.

1   Beethoven: Piano Sonata op. 10, no. 1 (third movement)

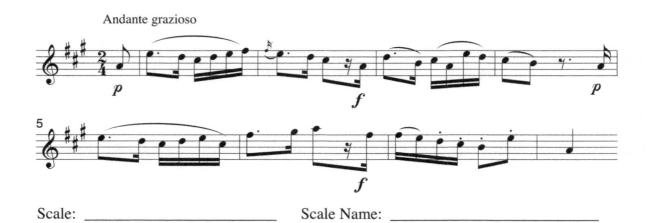

Scale: _____   Scale Name: _____

2   J. S. Bach: Sonata for Flute and Continuo, BWV 1034 (first movement)

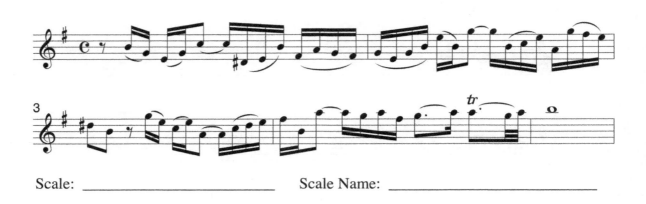

Scale: _____   Scale Name: _____

3   Mozart: Die Entführung aus dem Serail, K. 384 (act 2, no. 8)

Scale: _____   Scale Name: _____

4   Schumann: Symphonic Etudes, op. 13 (Theme)

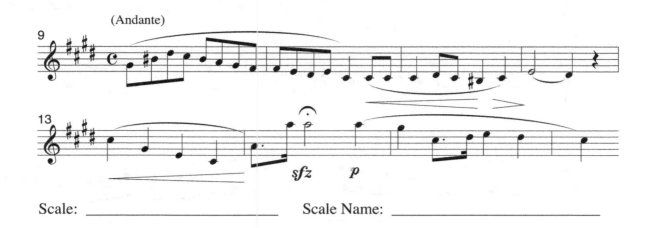

Scale: _____   Scale Name: _____

2H. The following melodies are based on the natural minor scale. Add the accidentals you would expect to find if the melodies were instead based on the melodic minor form. Remember that the sixth and seventh degrees normally are raised when their goal is the tonic and in their natural minor form when their goal is the dominant.

APPENDIX B

Rhythm

1. ELEMENTS OF THE PROPORTIONAL SYSTEM

1A. For each single note value, indicate how many of the specified smaller note types would have an equivalent duration.

1. 𝅝 = _____ ♩

2. 𝅝. = _____ ♩.

3. 𝅗𝅥. = _____ ♪.

4. 𝅗𝅥.. = _____ ♬

5. ♪ = _____ ♬

6. ♪. = _____ ♬

7. 𝅗𝅥.. = _____ ♬

8. 𝅝. = _____ 𝅗𝅥

9. 𝅗𝅥. = _____ ♪.

10. 𝅗𝅥. = _____ ♬

1B. Notate a single value equal to the combined value of those shown, using the fewest number of notes possible, along with ties and dots where necessary. In some cases, more than one possible answer exists.

1. ♩ ♩ ♪ ♬ _____

2. 𝅝 ♪ ♩ ♩ _____

3. ♪ ♪ ♪ 𝅗𝅥. _____

4. 𝅝 ♩ ♩ ♪ _____

5. 𝅗𝅥 ♩ 𝅗𝅥. ♬ _____

6. 𝅗𝅥 ♩ ♪ ♪ _____

7. ♩ ♬ 𝅗𝅥 𝅗𝅥 _____

8. ♪ 𝅗𝅥. 𝅗𝅥 𝅗𝅥 _____

9. ♬ ♬ ♬ ♪. _____

10. 𝅗𝅥. 𝅗𝅥. 𝅗𝅥 ♪ _____

1C. Notate the rhythm that compares to the given rhythm in the way specified.

1   Twice as long   _____

2   Half as long   _____

3   All note values 1½ their original value   _____

4   Three times as long   _____

5   Twice as long   _____

1D. Rewrite, replacing all dotted values with ties and all tied values with dotted values.

2. METER AND MEASURE

2A. Identify the accented notes in the melodies that follow, and indicate the type of accent (T for tonal, A for agogic, and D for dynamic) in each case.

1

2

2B. Draw the single note that represents the specified duration in the indicated meter.

1	$\frac{2}{3}$ beat	2	3 beats	3	3 beats	4	1 beat
	$\frac{6}{8}$		$\frac{3}{4}$		$\frac{5}{8}$		$\frac{9}{4}$

5	2 beats	6	$\frac{1}{4}$ beat	7	$\frac{1}{3}$ beat	8	$\frac{1}{4}$ beat
	$\frac{6}{4}$		$\frac{4}{4}$		$\frac{9}{8}$		$\frac{1}{2}$

2C. Indicate the precise value (the number of beats and fractional parts) spanned by each of the note values in the indicated meter.

1
$\frac{4}{4}$ 𝅗𝅥. = _____

2
$\frac{4}{2}$ 𝅗𝅥 𝅗𝅥. = _____

3
$\frac{9}{8}$ 𝅗𝅥. 𝅘𝅥 = _____

4
$\frac{3}{4}$ 𝅗𝅥. 𝅘𝅥. = _____

5
$\frac{6}{2}$ 𝅝. 𝅗𝅥. = _____

6
$\frac{6}{8}$ 𝅗𝅥. 𝅘𝅥𝅮 = _____

7
$\frac{5}{4}$ 𝅗𝅥. 𝅗𝅥. = _____

8
$\frac{4}{16}$ 𝅘𝅥 𝅘𝅥𝅮. = _____

9
$\frac{3}{2}$ 𝅝. 𝅗𝅥. = _____

10
$\frac{6}{4}$ 𝅗𝅥. 𝅗𝅥 𝅘𝅥𝅮 = _____

2D. Add bar lines to the following rhythmic passages.

2E. Each example contains an "over-filled' measure. Circle the single note that, if removed, will leave the proper number of beats.

2F. Notate this pattern:

in the following meters (some will require borrowed divisions):

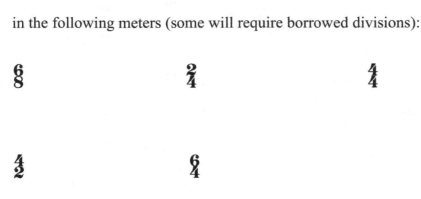

2G. Complete each measure by adding a single note value at the end.

3. NOTATING RHYTHM

3A. Using the fewest notes y, along with ties where needed, create a single duration lasting for the number of beats specified. Include bar lines where more than one measure is involved. Place fractional note values at the end.

1. meter: $\frac{9}{8}$ _____

$4\frac{2}{3}$ beats

2. meter: $\frac{4}{2}$ _____

$3\frac{1}{4}$ beats

3. meter: $\frac{12}{4}$ _____

$2\frac{1}{3}$ beats

4. meter: $\frac{6}{8}$ _____

$4\frac{1}{6}$ beats

5. meter: $\frac{4}{4}$ _____

$6\frac{3}{4}$ beats

6. meter: $\frac{3}{8}$ _____

$5\frac{1}{4}$ beats

7. meter: $\frac{5}{2}$ _____

$3\frac{1}{2}$ beats

8. meter: $\frac{3}{16}$ _____

$6\frac{1}{2}$ beats

9. meter: $\frac{6}{4}$ _____

$2\frac{1}{3}$ beats

10. meter: $\frac{4}{8}$ _____

$3\frac{1}{2}$ beats

3B. From the given list of meters, select the one that is most clearly reflected in each of the two-measure passages that follow. Each meter occurs at least once.

Meters: $\frac{3}{8}$ $\frac{5}{8}$ $\frac{6}{8}$ $\frac{9}{8}$ $\frac{3}{4}$ $\frac{6}{4}$ $\frac{3}{2}$ $\frac{4}{2}$

1

2

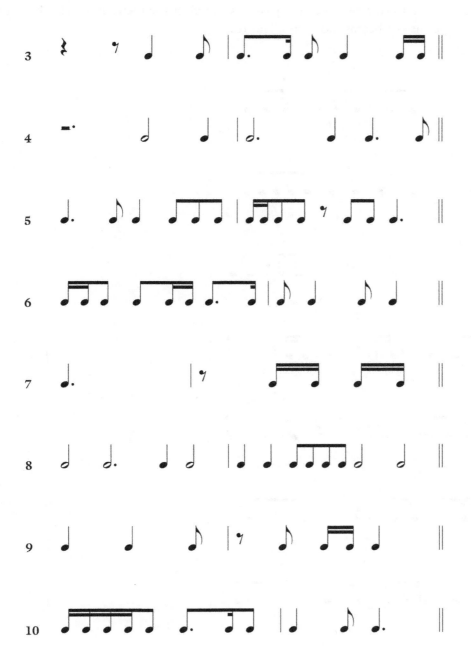

3C. Renotate each of the following two-measure passages to reflect the meter more clearly and to represent the proper use of beams, dots, ties, and rests.

3D. Above each of the following:

1. Replace the tied values with a single value where acceptable.

2. Renotate as tied values any dotted values that obscure the beat.

3. Renotate in equivalent values any rests at variance with accepted practice.

3E. Following are melodies from the literature. Using the clues to the meter provided by the notation and the directions for each, add a meter signature and bar lines. Assume that all begin with the first beat of the measure, unless otherwise indicated.

1   **Mozart: String Quartet K. 421 (fourth movement)**

First eighth note is an anacrusis; dotted quarter note = the beat

2   **Spiritual: "Swing Low Sweet Chariot"**

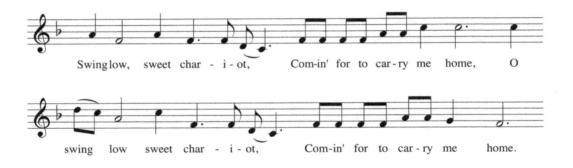

3   **Tartini: Sonata for Violin and Continuo (first movement)**

Dotted quarter note = the beat

4   Schubert: "Der Müller und der Bach" (from *Die Schöne Müllerin,* D. 795)

Dotted quarter note= the beat

Credits

"The Drums of Moria," from *Time Out of Mind: Six Tales for Middle Earth* by Daniel McCarthy. © 2006. Used by permission of C. Alan Publications

"Klavierstücke" op. 11, no. 1 by Arnold Schoenberg. Used by permission of Belmont Music Publishers.

CHAPTER THIRTY ONE

"Bluesette" by Norman Gimbel (words) and Jean Thielemans (music). © 1963, 1964 Songs of Universal, Inc. Copyright renewed; Words Renewed 1992 by Norman Gimbel for the world and assigned to Words West LLC (P.O. Box 15187, Beverly Hills, CA 90209 USA). All rights reserved. Used by permission. Reprinted with permission of Hal Leonard Corporation.

"Make Someone Happy," lyrics by Betty Comden and Adoph Green, and music by Jule Styne. © 1960 (renewed) Betty Comden, Adolph Green and Jule Styne Stratford Music Corp. All rights administered by Chappell & Co., Inc. All rights reserved. Used by permission.

"Prelude No. Two" Roland Hanna. Rahanna Music Inc. c/o 1630 Music Publishing Services, Inc. Reprinted with permission.

"Orbit" by Bill Evans. TRO—© Copyright 1967 (renewed) 1969 (renewed) Ludlow Music, Inc., New York, NY. International copyright secured. Made in USA. All rights reserved including public performance for profit. Used by permission.

"I Loves You Porgy" from *Porgy and Bess* by George Gershwin, Du Bose and Dorothy Heyward and Ira Gershwin. © 1935 (renewed) George Gershwin Music, Ira Gershwin Music and Du Bose and Dorothy Heyward Memorial Fund. All rights administered by WB Music Corp. All rights reserved. Used by permission

"The Birth of the Blues" by Ray Henderson (music) and B.G. DeSylva and Lew Brown (words). © 1926 (renewed) WB Music Corp., Ray Henderson Music and Stephen Ballentine Music. All rights reserved. Used by permission.

CHAPTER THIRTY TWO

"Straight, No Chaser" by Thelonius Monk. © 1962 (Renewed 1990) by Thelonius Music Corp. International copyright secured. All rights reserved. Reprinted with permission of Hal Leonard Corporation.